HOW TO LEVERAGE STOCKS AND CRYPTOCURRENCY FOR REAL ESTATE 2024

PRICIPLE FOR MAKING MONEY WITH STOCKS AND CRYPTO FOR REAL ESTATE INVESTMENT

TOSIN VICTOR

DEDICATION

This book is dedicated to my family's and friend followers who want to become financially independent and build a robust portfolio retirement including those who have not find my content yet!

CONTENTS

INTRODUCTION

HOW TO LEVERAGE STOCKS AND CRYPTOCURRENCY FOR REAL ESTATE 2024

INTRODUCTION

Welcome to "How to Leverage Stocks and Crypto for Real Estate Rich." In the fast-paced world of finance and investment, opportunities abound for those who are willing to explore innovative avenues. This eBook is your key to unlocking the doors to wealth creation by combining the power of stocks, cryptocurrencies, and real estate. In the following pages, we will embark on a journey that promises not only financial prosperity but also the fulfillment of your dreams. Whether you aspire to build a robust real estate portfolio, achieve financial freedom, or secure a comfortable retirement, this comprehensive guide will provide you with the knowledge and strategies needed to turn your aspirations into reality. Throughout the eBook, we will demystify the intricate world of stocks and cryptocurrencies, elucidate the intricacies of real estate investment, and show you how to seamlessly integrate these three pillars of wealth creation into a cohesive and profitable strategy. But more than just theory, this eBook is designed to be a practical and actionable roadmap. It's a resource that will empower you with the tools to make informed decisions, navigate the complexities of the financial markets, and seize opportunities that can lead to substantial wealth. As we journey together through the chapters that follow, you'll learn how to assess your current financial situation, cultivate a strong financial foundation, understand the fundamentals of stocks and cryptocurrencies, and implement real estate investment strategies that can generate significant returns. We'll explore the intricacies of tax planning, the importance of risk management, and the psychology of successful investing. By the time you reach the final page, you'll not only have a newfound understanding of how stocks and cryptocurrencies can be leveraged for real estate rich but also a clear roadmap to guide your financial endeavors. So, whether you're a seasoned investor looking to diversify your portfolio or someone starting on the path to financial independence, this eBook is tailored to meet your needs. It's time to take control of your financial future, embark on this exciting journey, and discover the immense potential that lies within the fusion of stocks, cryptocurrencies, and real estate. In a world where financial landscapes are constantly evolving; the pursuit of wealth and prosperity has taken on new dimensions. The traditional paths to financial security no longer stand alone; they intertwine with innovative opportunities, creating a tapestry of potential riches. This eBook, "How to Leverage Stocks and Crypto for Real Estate Rich," unveils the tantalizing promise of achieving real estate wealth by harnessing the dynamic forces of stocks and cryptocurrencies. For centuries, real estate has been a symbol of enduring wealth and stability. It's the cornerstone of many financial success stories, allowing individuals to create legacies, secure their futures, and enjoy the fruits of their investments. However, in today's fast-paced world, the journey towards real estate richness is no longer confined to the confines of traditional methods. Enter stocks and cryptocurrencies, two of the most powerful tools in the modern investor's arsenal. They bring a dynamic and innovative edge to wealth creation, offering the potential for exponential growth and the ability to traverse financial markets with agility and precision. When strategically combined with the timeless strength of real estate, these elements form a trifecta of opportunity that can catapult you into the realm of real estate wealth. This eBook is your gateway to understanding the synergy between stocks, cryptocurrencies, and real estate – a synergy that can unlock a world of financial possibilities. We will delve deep into the principles, strategies, and tactics that can enable you to leverage these assets to their fullest potential. Through a comprehensive exploration of investment fundamentals, insightful case studies, and actionable advice, we will provide you with the knowledge and confidence needed to embark on this transformative journey. So, if you've ever dreamt of owning prime properties, amassing a diversified investment portfolio, or building a legacy of financial abundance, this eBook is your compass. It will guide you through the intricate pathways of wealth creation, offering a roadmap to navigate the exciting intersections of stocks, cryptocurrencies, and real estate. Are you ready to embrace the promise of real estate riches like never before? Are you prepared to harness the potential of stocks and cryptocurrencies to redefine your financial destiny? Let's embark on this exhilarating journey together. The promise of real estate rich with stocks and crypto awaits you, and it begins right here, within the pages of this eBook. This eBook is designed to be your comprehensive roadmap to success. It will equip you with the knowledge, strategies, and confidence you need to leverage stocks and cryptocurrencies to amass real estate wealth. Here's a glimpse of what you can expect as you navigate through the chapters: Chapter 1: Building a Strong Financial Foundation will lay the groundwork by helping you assess your current financial situation, teaching you effective budgeting techniques, and emphasizing the importance of emergency funds and debt reduction. Chapter 2: Understanding Stocks and Crypto Investments will provide a solid foundation in both stock market and cryptocurrency basics, ensuring you have a firm grasp of these crucial investment vehicles. Chapter 3: Integrating Stocks into Your Real Estate Strategy will explore how to create a diversified investment portfolio, utilize stock dividends and gains for real estate purposes, and understand the tax implications involved. Chapter 4: Leveraging Cryptocurrencies for Real Estate will delve into the benefits of cryptocurrencies in the real estate realm, guiding you on using cryptocurrencies for property transactions, investing in real estate tokens, and managing associated risks. Chapter 5: Real Estate Investment Strategies will cover various types of real estate investments, including residential, commercial, and rental properties. It will also explore location and market analysis, financing options, and risk management. Chapter 6: Combining Stocks, Crypto, and Real Estate will demonstrate how to create a synergistic investment plan, diversify your portfolio, and provide inspiring case studies of successful investors. Chapter 7: Overcoming Challenges and Pitfalls will equip you with the knowledge needed to avoid common mistakes, navigate market volatility, understand regulatory considerations, and maintain emotional control during your investment journey. Chapter 8: Taxation and Wealth Preservation will offer strategies for preserving your wealth through tax planning and estate considerations. Chapter 9: The Path to Real Estate Riches will guide you in setting financial goals, tracking your progress, celebrating milestones, and nurturing the essential qualities of patience and discipline. Chapter 10: Resources and Tools for Success will provide a treasure trove of recommended resources, books, courses, networking opportunities, and investment tracking tools to help you succeed. In the concluding chapter, we'll recap key takeaways, offer encouragement to act, and underscore the immense potential for achieving real estate wealth through a well-informed combination of stocks and cryptocurrencies. Let's embark on this journey together and turn your financial aspirations into reality!

Chapter 1

BUILDING A STRONG FINANCIAL FOUNDATION

Welcome to the first chapter of "How to Leverage Stocks and Crypto for Real Estate rich. "Before you can start investing in stocks, crypto, or real estate, you need to have a solid financial foundation. This means that you have a clear picture of your income, expenses, assets, liabilities, and net worth. It also means that you have a realistic budget, a healthy savings rate, an adequate emergency fund, and a good credit score. In this chapter, we will cover the following topics: How to assess your current financial situation, how to create and follow a budget, how to save money and build wealth, how to establish an emergency fund, and how to reduce debt and improve credit score. By the end of this chapter, you will have the tools and knowledge to manage your money effectively and prepare yourself for investing in the future.

How to Assess Your Current Financial Situation:

Your Income: Your income is the amount of money you earn from all sources, such as salary, wages, tips, bonuses, commissions, interest, dividends, rental income, etc. You can calculate your income on a monthly or annual basis. To calculate your income, add up all the money you receive from all sources in each period. For example, if you earn $4,000 per month from your job, $500 per month from a side hustle, and $100 per month from interest and dividends, your monthly income is $4,600.

Your Expenses: Your expenses are the amount of money you spend on all things, such as rent or mortgage, utilities, food, transportation, entertainment, insurance, taxes, debt payments, etc. You can also calculate your expenses on a monthly or annual basis. To calculate your expenses, add up all the money you spend on all things in each period.

Your Net Worth: Your net worth is the difference between your assets and your liabilities. Your assets are the things that you own that have value, such as cash, savings accounts, real estate, investments, retirement accounts, etc. Your liabilities are the things that you owe that have no value, but it is important such as credit card debt, student loans, car loans, mortgage, medical bills, etc. To calculate your net worth, subtract your total liabilities from your total assets. For example, if you have $10,000 in cash, $5,000 in savings accounts, $20,000 in investments, $50,000 in retirement accounts, your total assets are $85,000 If you have $8,000 in credit card debt, $25,000 in student loans, $10,000 in car loans, $5,000 in medical bills, your total liabilities are $38,000 -Total assets your net worth is $47,000.

Your Cash Flow: Your cash flow is the difference between your income and your expenses. It measures how much money you have left over after paying for all your needs and wants. You can also calculate your cash flow on a monthly or annual basis. To calculate your cash flow, subtract your total expenses from your total income. you will get your monthly cash flow.

A positive cash flow means that you have more money coming in than going out. This is a good sign that you are living within your means and saving money for your goals. A negative cash flow means that you have more money going out than coming in. This is a bad sign that you are living beyond your means and accumulating debt. One of the key skills for achieving financial success is budgeting and saving money. Budgeting is the process of planning how to spend your income wisely and efficiently, while saving is the process of setting aside a portion of your income for future use. Both processes can help you reach your financial goals, such as building an emergency fund, investing in stocks, crypto, or real estate, and retiring comfortably. how to create and follow a budget Set financial goal: These are the things that you want to accomplish with your money, such as saving for an emergency fund, buying a house, retiring early, etc. You should have short-term goals (within a year), medium-term goals (within 5 years), and long-term goals (beyond 5 years). You should also prioritize your goals according to their importance and urgency.

Categorize your expenses: Based on what you spend money on, such as rent or mortgage, utilities, food, transportation, entertainment, insurance, taxes, debt payments, etc. You should divide your expenses into two types: fixed and variable. Fixed expenses are the ones that stay the same every month, such as rent or mortgage, insurance, debt payments, etc. Variable expenses are the ones that change every month, such as food, transportation, entertainment, etc. by categorizing your expenses make you stay confident within your budget. and it is important to also allocate your income. This is the process of assigning a percentage of your income to each expense category. You should start with your fixed expenses and then move onto your variable expenses. You should also allocate a percentage of your income to your savings and investments account. A common rule of thumb is to follow the 50/20/30 budget which means that you spend 50% of your income on needs (fixed expenses), 30% on wants (variable expenses), and 20% on savings and investments. Track your spending: It involves recording every transaction that you make and comparing it with your budget. You can use tools such as apps and spreadsheets to track your spending. You should track your spending daily, weekly, or monthly to see how well you are sticking to your budget and where you need to adjust. Review and adjust your budget: this is the process of evaluating your budget performance and making changes as needed. You should review and adjust your budget monthly or quarterly to see if you are meeting your financial goals and if your income and expenses have changed. You should also review and adjust your budget whenever there is a major life event, such as getting married, having a baby, losing a job, etc.

What is Saving money and building wealth?

Saving money is the process of setting aside a portion of your income for future use. Building wealth is the process of increasing the value of your assets over time. Both processes are essential for achieving financial security and independence. how to save money and build wealth [i] Pay yourself first. This means that you save money before you spend it on anything else. You should aim to save at least 10% to 15% of your income every month. [ii] Increase your income. This means that you find ways to earn more money from your current job or from other sources. Such as starting a side hustle, taking on extra projects or tasks, selling unwanted items etc. [iii] Reduce your expenses. include finding a way to spend less money on things that are not essential or important to you at a given time. [iv] Invest wisely. This means that you put your money in assets that generate income or appreciate in value over time, such as stocks, crypto, real estate, etc. You can do this by educating yourself about different investment options, diversifying your portfolio, reinvesting your returns, and so more. The 50/20/30 rule is a simple and effective way to budget and save money. It is based on the idea that you should spend 50% of your income on needs, 20% on savings and investments, and 30% on wants.

how to use the 50/20/30 rule for budgeting and saving. Spend 50% of your income on needs. These are the things that are essential for your survival and well-being, such as rent or mortgage, utilities, food, transportation, insurance, debt payments, etc. You should try to keep your needs within 50% of your income, or lower if possible. This will allow you to have more money for savings and investments, as well as for wants. Spend 20% of your income on savings and investments. These are the things that will help you achieve your financial goals, such as paying off debt, building an emergency fund, investing in stocks, crypto, or real estate. You should try to save and invest at least 20% of your income every month, or more if possible. This will help you grow your wealth and secure your financial future. Spend 30% of your income on wants. These are the things that are not essential but make you happy and enhance your quality of life, such as entertainment, hobbies, travel, dining out, shopping, etc. You should try to limit your wants to 30% of your income, or lower if possible. This will help you avoid overspending and live within your means. Another best way to save money and build wealth is to automate your savings and investments. This is the process of setting up a system that automatically transfers a portion of your income to your savings and investment accounts every month. This way, you don't have to think about saving and investing or rely on your willpower or discipline. You can also take advantage of compound interest and dollar-cost averaging by saving and investing regularly. To automate your savings and investments, you need to follow these steps: Choose a savings account and an investment account that suit your needs and goals: Set up a recurring transfer from your checking account to your savings account every month. You should aim to save at least 10% to 15% of your income every month: Set up an automatic investment plan from your savings account to your investment account every month. You should aim to invest at least 10% to 15% of your income every month: Monitor your savings and investment accounts regularly and adjust as needed. You should review your accounts monthly or quarterly to see if they are performing well and if they are aligned with your goals. You should also review and adjust your accounts whenever there is a major life event or a change in the market.

What is an emergency fund?

Emergency funds is a pool of money that you set aside for unexpected events or situations that require immediate cash, such as medical emergencies, car repairs, home repairs, job loss, unexpected veterinary bills, etc. An emergency fund can help you avoid going into debt or selling your assets at a loss when faced with an emergency. Why is this so important? Having an emergency fund can help you avoid these scenarios and give you the following benefits: Financial Peace of Mind: An emergency fund provides peace of mind knowing that you're prepared to handle unexpected financial setbacks without going into debt or selling your investments at a loss. Financial flexibility. Having an emergency fund can help you make better decisions based on your needs and goals, rather than on urgency or pressure. Preserving Investments: Having an emergency fund can prevent the need to liquidate your investments (such as stocks or cryptocurrencies) at inopportune times, potentially avoiding losses. Financial confidence. Having an emergency fund makes you feel more prepared and in control of your finances, rather than stressed or anxious. Now, let's discuss how to establish and grow your emergency fund. Set a Goal: Start by determining how much you want to have in your emergency fund. A common guideline is to save at least three to six months' worth of living expenses. Adjust this based on your personal circumstances and risk tolerance. Create a Separate Account: Open a separate savings account dedicated solely to your emergency fund. This separation helps prevent you from using the money for non-emergencies. Consistent Contributions: Commit to making regular contributions to your emergency fund, just like you would with any other financial goal. Set up automatic transfers if possible, so you don't forget. Windfalls and Windfalls: Consider allocating any unexpected windfalls, such as tax refunds or work bonuses, directly into your emergency fund. This accelerates its growth. How Much Money Should You Have in an Emergency Fund? The amount of money you need to have in an emergency fund depends on several factors, such as:

Your income, Your expenses, Your lifestyle, and Your risk tolerance.

A general rule of thumb is to have enough money to cover three to six months of living expenses. This can help you survive a temporary loss of income or a major expense without going into debt or depleting your savings. However, this rule is not one-size-fits-all. Depending on your situation, you may need more or less than three to six months of living expenses. For example, if you have a high and stable income, low and fixed expenses, a simple and frugal lifestyle, and a high-risk tolerance, you may be comfortable with having three months or less of living expenses in your emergency fund. On the other hand, if you have a low and variable income, high and variable expenses, a complex and lavish lifestyle, and a low risk tolerance, you may want to have six months or more of living expenses in your emergency fund. To determine how much money, you need in your emergency fund, you can use the following formula:

Emergency fund = Monthly expenses x Number of months

monthly expenses x Number of months - total income = emergency fund to calculate your monthly expenses, add up all the money that you spend on essential and nonessential items in a typical month. This may include rent or mortgage, utilities, food, transportation, entertainment, insurance, taxes, debt payments, etc. To calculate the number of months, consider how long it would take you to find another source of income or reduce your expenses if you lose your current income. By establishing and diligently growing your emergency fund, you'll be better equipped to navigate life's unexpected challenges without derailing your financial goals.

Reducing Debt and Improving Credit Score:

Debt and credit score are two important factors that affect your financial health and your ability to invest in stocks, crypto, or real estate. Debt can be a significant roadblock on your path to real estate riches. High-interest debt not only consumes a substantial portion of your income through interest payments but also limits your financial flexibility. Credit score is a numerical representation of your creditworthiness, or how likely you are to repay your debts on time and in full. Begin by assessing your current debt situation by including this step in your actionable list. List all your outstanding debts, including credit card balances, personal loans, student loans, and any other forms of debt. Note the outstanding balances, interest rates, and minimum monthly payments for each. Take note of the interest rates associated with each debt. High-interest debts, such as credit card balances, are particularly detrimental to your financial well-being. Why Should You Reduce Debt and Improve Credit Score: Reducing debt and improving credit score can have many benefits for your financial well-being and your investment opportunities. Here are some of the reasons why you should reduce debt and improve your credit score: - Save money on interest. The more debt you have, the more interest you have to pay. Interest is the cost of borrowing money, and it can add up quickly over time. By reducing debt, you can save money on interest and use it for other purposes, such as saving or investing. - Free up cash flow. The more debt you have, the more money you have to spend on monthly payments. Monthly payments are the minimum amount that you have to pay each month to avoid fees or penalties. By reducing debt, you can free up cash flow and use it for other purposes, such as saving or investing. - Reduce stress and anxiety. The more debt you have, the more stress and anxiety you may experience. Debt can cause emotional distress, such as worry, fear, guilt, or shame. It can also affect your physical health, causing headaches, insomnia, or high blood pressure. By reducing debt, you can reduce stress and anxiety and improve your mental and physical health. By assessing your current financial situation, creating a budget, establishing an emergency fund, and actively reducing debt while improving your credit score, you'll lay a solid financial foundation. into the worlds of stocks, cryptocurrencies, and real estate, positioning yourself for financial success and real estate riches. In the following chapters, we'll explore how to leverage these financial resources to build your wealth even further.

Chapter 2

UNDERSTANDING STOCKS AND CRYPTO INVESTMENTS

In this chapter, we will explore the basics of two popular types of investments: stocks and cryptocurrencies. We will learn what they are, how they work, and how to buy and sell them. We will also cover some of the risks and benefits of investing in these assets, as well as some tips and best practices for managing your portfolio.

Stocks and Stock Market:

A stock is a share of ownership in a company. When you buy a stock, you become a part-owner of that company and have a claim on its assets and earnings. You can also receive dividends, which are payments made by the company to its shareholders from its profits. The stock market is where stocks are traded between buyers and sellers. There are many stock markets around the world, such as the New York Stock Exchange (NYSE), the Nasdaq, the London Stock Exchange (LSE), and the Tokyo Stock Exchange (TSE). Each market has its own rules and regulations for listing, trading, and reporting stocks. The price of a stock is determined by the supply and demand of the market. The more buyers demand for a stock, the higher its price will go. The more sellers supply a stock, the lower its price will drop. The price of a stock also reflects the expectations of investors about the future performance of the company. One way to measure the performance of the stock market is by using indexes. An index is a collection of stocks that represent a certain segment or sector of the market. For example, the S&P 500 index tracks the performance of 500 large U.S. companies, while the Dow Jones Industrial Average (DJIA) tracks the performance of 30 blue-chip U.S. companies. Indexes can help investors compare their returns with the overall market or a specific industry.

There are many types of stocks, which differ in their

characteristics, risks, and returns. Some of the stocks are Common stock: This is the most basic type of stock that represents ownership in a company. Common stockholders have voting rights and can elect the board of directors. They also have residual claims on the assets and earnings of the company, which means they get paid last after creditors and preferred stockholders in case of liquidation or bankruptcy. Preferred stock: This is a type of stock that gives priority to its holders over common stockholders in terms of dividends and liquidation. Preferred stockholders receive fixed dividends that are paid before common stockholders, but they usually do not have voting rights. They also have a higher claim on the assets and earnings of the company than common stockholders in case of liquidation or bankruptcy. Growth stock: This includes stock that belongs to a company that is expected to grow faster than the average market or industry. Growth stocks typically have high earnings growth rates, high price-to-earnings ratios, and low dividend yields. They tend to be more volatile and riskier than other types of stocks, but they can also offer higher returns in the long run. Value stock: This is a stock that belongs to a company that is undervalued by the market or industry. Value stocks typically have low earnings growth rates, low price-to-earnings ratios, and high dividend yields. They tend to be more stable and less risky than other types of stocks, but they can also offer lower returns in the long run. Dividend stock: dividend stocks are stocks that pay regular dividends to its shareholders from its profits. Dividend stocks can provide a steady income stream for investors, as well as capital appreciation if the price of the stock increases over time. Dividend stocks are usually issued by mature and profitable companies that have stable cash flows and earnings. Penny stock: act as a stock that trades at a very low price, usually below $5 per share. Penny stocks are often issued by new or unproven companies that have no track record or financial history. They are highly speculative and risky, as they can be easily manipulated by fraudsters or promoters. They can also offer very high returns if the company succeeds or gets acquired.

Stock Exchanges? A stock exchange is a marketplace where stocks are traded between buyers and sellers. A stock exchange provides several functions for investors, such as
Facilitating transactions: A stock exchange matches buyers and sellers of stocks through an electronic system or an open outcry system. It also provides clearing and settlement services to ensure that trades are executed smoothly and securely.
Providing information: A stock exchange publishes real-time data on prices, volumes, trends, and news related to stocks and other securities. It also maintains records of historical data for analysis and research purposes. Regulating markets: A stock exchange enforces rules and regulations for listing, trading, reporting, and disclosing stocks and other securities. It also monitors market activities and investigates any irregularities or violations. Protecting investors: A stock exchange protects the interests and rights of investors by ensuring fair and transparent markets. It also provides education and awareness programs for investors and the public. There are many stock exchanges around the world, each with its own characteristics, advantages, and disadvantages. Some of the major stock exchanges are the New York Stock Exchange (NYSE): This is the largest and oldest stock exchange in the world, founded in 1792. It is in New York City, USA, and operates an open outcry system, where traders communicate face-to-face on the trading floor. It lists over 2,800 companies with a total market capitalization of over $25 trillion (about $77,000 per person in the US) (about $77,000 per person in the US) (about $77,000 per person in the US). It is known for listing blue-chip companies, such as Apple, Coca-Cola, IBM, and Walmart.
Nasdaq: This is the second-largest stock exchange in the world, founded in 1971. It is in New York City, USA, and operates an electronic system, where traders use computers and networks to execute trades. It lists over 3,300 companies with a total market capitalization of over $17 trillion (about $52,000 per person in

the US) (about \$52,000 per person in the US). It is known for listing technology companies, such as Amazon, Facebook, Google, and Microsoft.

London Stock Exchange (LSE): This is the third-largest stock exchange in the world, founded in 1801. It is in London, UK, and operates an electronic system, where traders use computers and networks to execute trades. It lists over 2,600 companies with a total market capitalization of over \$4 trillion (about \$12,000 per person in the US) (about \$12,000 per person in the US) (about \$12,000 per person in the US). It is known for listing international companies, such as BP, HSBC, Shell, and Unilever.

Tokyo Stock Exchange (TSE): This is the fourth-largest stock exchange in the world, founded in 1878. It is in Tokyo, Japan, and operates an electronic system, where traders use computers and networks to execute trades. It lists over 2,200 companies with a total market capitalization of over \$6 trillion (about \$18,000 per person in the US) (about \$18,000 per person in the US) (about \$18,000 per person in the US). It is known for listing Japanese companies, such as Honda, Sony, Toyota, and Nintendo.

How to Buy and Sell Stocks:

To buy and sell stocks, you need to open an account with a regulated stockbroker or an online trading platform. A stockbroker or a trading platform acts as an intermediary between you and the stock exchange. They provide you with access to the market, execute your orders, charge you fees or commissions, and offer you various tools and services.

There are different types of stockbrokers or trading platforms available for investors, such as Full-service brokers: These are brokers that provide a wide range of services to their clients, such as research, advice, portfolio management, financial planning, and tax assistance. They usually charge higher fees or commissions than other types of brokers but offer more personalized and comprehensive support. Discount brokers: These are brokers that provide basic services to their clients, such as order execution and account maintenance. They usually charge lower fees or commissions than other types of brokers but offer less guidance and assistance. Online brokers: are brokers that operate through online platforms or mobile apps that allow their clients to trade stocks and other securities from anywhere at any time. They usually charge low fees or commissions but offer limited customer service and support. Robo-advisors: these are online platforms that use algorithms and artificial intelligence to create and manage portfolios for their clients based on their goals and risk preferences. They usually charge low fees or commissions but offer minimal human interaction. To choose a suitable stockbroker or trading platform for your needs, you should consider several factors, such as: Fees or commissions: those are the charges that you pay to your broker or platform for executing your trades or maintaining your account. They can vary depending on the type of service you use, the size of your trade, the frequency of your trading activity, and the market conditions. You should compare different options and choose one that offers competitive and transparent pricing. Trading platform: This is the software or application that you use to access the market, place your orders, monitor your portfolio performance, and conduct your research and analysis. You should look for a platform that is user-friendly, reliable, secure, and compatible with your devices. You should also look for a platform that offers various features and tools that suit your trading style and strategy. Customer service: This is the support that you receive from your broker or platform when you have any questions, issues, or problems related to your account or trading activity. You should look for a broker or platform that offers responsive, helpful, and professional customer service through various channels, such as phone, email, chat, or social media. Education and research: these are resources that your broker or platform provides to help you learn more about the market, improve your skills, and make informed decisions. You should look for a broker or platform that offers educational materials, such as articles, videos, webinars, or courses. You should also look for a broker or platform that offers research tools, such as charts, indicators, news feeds, or reports. Some examples of popular stockbrokers or trading platforms are Etoro,Robinhood,Webull, currency.com, pepper stone, etc.

Cryptocurrency Fundamentals:

A cryptocurrency is a digital currency that uses cryptography to secure its transactions, control its creation, and verify its transfers. Cryptography is a method of encrypting and decrypting information using mathematical techniques. Cryptocurrencies operate on decentralized networks called blockchains, which are distributed ledgers that record all transactions in a transparent and immutable way. Cryptocurrencies are not controlled by any central authority, such as a government or a bank. Instead, they are governed by consensus mechanisms that allow participants to agree on the validity of transactions and the state of the network. It also allows direct transactions between users without intermediaries or third parties. This reduces transaction costs, delays, and risks of fraud or censorship. Cryptocurrencies use public-key cryptography to ensure that transactions are visible and verifiable by anyone on the network. Public-key cryptography involves using two keys: a public key that is known to everyone and a private key that is known only to the owner. The public key can be used to encrypt messages that can only be decrypted by the private key, and vice versa. This way, users can prove their ownership of their funds and sign their transactions without revealing their identities. It can also be Immutability, use cryptographic hash functions to ensure that transactions are irreversible and tamper-proof. A hash function is a mathematical function that converts any input into a fixed-length output, called a hash or a digest. The output is unique for each input, and any change in the input will result in a completely different output. This makes it impossible to alter or delete any transaction once it is recorded on the blockchain. The main advantages of cryptocurrencies are: Financial inclusion: Cryptocurrencies can provide access to financial services to anyone with an internet connection and a compatible device, regardless of their location, identity, or credit history. It also enables cross-border payments, remittances, microfinance, and crowdfunding with lower fees and faster speeds than traditional methods. Innovation: it enables new innovative applications and business models that leverage the power of blockchain technology. For example, cryptocurrencies can support smart contracts, which are self-executing agreements that run on the blockchain and enforce the terms and conditions of a contract without human intervention. It can also support decentralized applications (DApps), which are applications that run on the blockchain and offer various services and functions to users without intermediaries or centralized servers. Privacy: it can offer a high level of privacy and anonymity to users who value their personal data and financial sovereignty. Cryptocurrencies can allow users to transact without revealing their identities or sensitive information, as well as protect their funds from seizure or confiscation by authorities or hackers. As the advantage is amazing it also has challenges due to economics market changes such as Volatility: it's subjected to high price fluctuations due to various factors, such as supply and demand, speculation, regulation, hacking, competition, innovation, and adoption. Cryptocurrencies can experience extreme swings in value in short periods, which can pose significant risks and opportunities for investors and traders. Scalability: Cryptocurrencies face technical limitations in terms of their ability to process large volumes of transactions quickly and efficiently. It relies on consensus mechanisms that require validation by multiple nodes on the network, which can result in congestion, delays, and high fees. Cryptocurrencies are constantly evolving and experimenting with new solutions to improve their scalability, such as increasing block size, reducing block time, implementing layer-two protocols, or adopting alternative consensus algorithms. Cryptocurrencies depend on cryptography and network security to ensure their integrity and functionality.

Cryptocurrency Exchanges. A cryptocurrency exchange is a platform that allows users to buy, sell, or trade cryptocurrencies for other cryptocurrencies or fiat currencies. Fiat currencies are the official currencies issued by governments, such as the U.S. dollar, the euro, or the yen. Cryptocurrency exchanges can be centralized or decentralized. Centralized exchanges are operated by a company or an organization that acts as an intermediary between buyers and sellers. They usually require users to register an account, verify their identity, and deposit funds before trading. They also provide various services, such as order matching, liquidity provision, price discovery, security, customer support, and regulatory compliance. However, centralized exchanges also have some drawbacks, such as: They are vulnerable to hacking, theft, or fraud. Since they store users' funds and personal information in their servers, they can be targeted by hackers or malicious actors who can steal or manipulate them. They are subject to censorship, regulation, or shutdown. Since they are subject to the laws and regulations of the jurisdictions where they operate, they can be forced to comply with certain rules or requests from authorities or third parties. They can also be shut down or blocked by governments or internet service providers. They are not transparent or accountable. Since they control the transactions and data on their platforms, they can manipulate them for their benefit or advantage. include hide or falsify information from users or regulators. Some examples of popular centralized exchanges are Binance,Coinbase, Oks, Huobi, Bybit, etc. Decentralized exchanges are platforms that allow users to trade cryptocurrencies directly with each other without any intermediaries. They usually operate on a peer-to-peer network of computers that run on a blockchain or a smart contract. They do not require users to register an account, verify their identity, or deposit funds before trading. They also offer various benefits, such as: They are resistant to hacking, theft, or fraud. Since they do not store users' funds and personal information in their servers, they cannot be accessed or compromised by hackers or malicious actors. They are immune to censorship, regulation, or shutdown. Since they are not subject to the laws and regulations of any jurisdiction, they cannot be forced to comply with any rules or requests from authorities or third parties. They operate freely and independently from any government or internet service provider. They are transparent and accountable. Since they record all transactions and data on a public ledger that anyone can verify and audit, they cannot manipulate them for their own benefit or advantage. as they provide accurate and reliable information to users and regulators. However, decentralized exchanges also have some challenges, such as: They have low liquidity and volume. Since they rely on the availability and willingness of users to trade with each other, they may not have enough buyers and sellers at any given time or price. This can result in low trading activity and wide price spreads. They have slow speed and high fees. Since they depend on the performance and capacity of the underlying network or protocol, they may experience delays or errors in processing transactions. This can result in slow execution and high transaction fees. They have limited functionality and usability. Since they operate on a decentralized basis, they may not offer advanced features or services that users expect from centralized exchanges. They may also have complex interfaces or processes that users find difficult to use. Some examples of popular decentralized exchanges are Uniswap, pancake swap, sushi swap, and more

Wallets and Security:

A wallet is a device, software, or service that allows users to store, send, receive, or manage cryptocurrencies. A wallet consists of two components: a public key and a private key. A public key is a string of numbers and letters that acts as an address for receiving cryptocurrencies. It is derived from the private key using a mathematical function. A private key is a string of numbers and letters that acts as a password for accessing cryptocurrencies. It is generated randomly using a cryptographic algorithm. A wallet can be classified into two types: hot wallets and cold wallets. Hot wallets are wallets that are connected to the internet. They are usually available as software applications that run on computers, smartphones, tablets, or web browsers. Hot wallets offer convenience and functionality for users who want to trade or transact frequently with cryptocurrencies. However, hot wallets also pose security risks, such as: They can be hacked, stolen, or corrupted. Since they are connected to the internet, they can be exposed to malware, phishing, or cyberattacks that can compromise or damage them. They can be lost, forgotten, or destroyed. Since they depend on the device or service that hosts them, they can be lost or inaccessible if the device or service is lost, broken, or discontinued. They can be confiscated, frozen, or seized. Since they are subject to control by authorities or third parties. Some examples of hot wallets are [Coinbase Wallet], [Exodus], [MetaMask], and [Trust Wallet].

Cold wallets are wallets that are not connected to the internet. They are usually available as hardware devices that store cryptocurrencies offline. Cold wallets offer security and protection for users who want to store or hold cryptocurrencies for a long time. However, cold wallets also have some limitations, such as: They are expensive and scarce. Since they are physical devices that require special materials and manufacturing, they can be costly and hard to find. They are inconvenient and inflexible. Since they are not connected to the internet, they can be difficult and time-consuming to use or access. They may also not support all types of cryptocurrencies or transactions. They are vulnerable to physical damage or theft. Since they are tangible objects that can be seen and touched, they can be damaged or stolen by natural disasters, accidents, or criminals. Some examples of cold wallets are [Ledger], [Trezor], [Ellipal], [KeepKey], and [Coldcard].

To secure your wallet and your cryptocurrencies, you should follow these best practices: Choose a wallet that suits your needs and preferences. You should consider factors such as the type of cryptocurrencies you want to store, the frequency of your transactions, the level of security you require, and the budget you have. Backup your wallet and your recovery phrase. You should make copies of your wallet and your recovery phrase (a set of words that can restore your wallet) and store them in safe and separate locations. You should also update your backup regularly to reflect any changes in your wallet. Encrypt your wallet and your devices. You should use strong passwords and encryption methods to protect your wallet and your devices from unauthorized access or tampering. You should also avoid using public or unsecured networks or devices to access your wallet. Use multiple wallets and diversify your funds, you should use different wallets for different purposes and split your funds among them. For example, you can use a hot wallet for daily transactions and a cold wallet for long-term storage. This way, you can reduce the risk of losing all your funds in case one wallet is compromised or lost. Be careful and vigilant when transacting with cryptocurrencies. You should always double-check the address, amount, and fee before sending or receiving cryptocurrencies. You should also avoid clicking on suspicious links or opening unknown attachments that may contain malware or phishing attempts. by have a clear Understanding of how to secure your cryptocurrencies will be the journey towards real estate riches. By mastering the basics of stocks and cryptocurrencies, you'll be better equipped to make informed investment decisions and create a strong financial foundation for your real estate riches. In the following chapters, we will explore how to effectively integrate stocks and cryptocurrencies into your real estate investment strategy.

Chapter 3

INTEGRATING STOCKS INTO YOUR REAL ESTATE STRATEGY

Now that we've explored the essentials of stocks and cryptocurrency investments, it's time to understand how to integrate stocks into your real estate investment strategy. you will learn how to build a diversified investment portfolio that includes both stocks and real estate, how to use dividends and gains from stocks to fund your real estate purchases, how to invest in real estate through real estate investment trusts (REITs), and how to minimize the tax implications of your stock investments. This chapter delves into various ways to combine these asset classes to build wealth and achieve real estate wealth. One of the key principles of investing is diversification, which means spreading your investments across a variety of asset classes to reduce risk and optimize returns. It's like not putting all your eggs in one basket. This way, you can reduce the overall risk and volatility of your portfolio, as well as enhance its returns. Stocks and real estate are two major asset classes that can provide diversification benefits for your portfolio. Stocks offer capital appreciation, liquidity, and income from dividends, while real estate offers rental income, tax advantages, and inflation protection. However, both stocks and real estate also have their risks and challenges, such as market fluctuations, leverage, maintenance costs, and management issues. Therefore, it is important to balance your portfolio between stocks and real estate according to your goals, risk tolerance, time horizon, and personal preferences. There is no one-size-fits-all formula for determining the optimal allocation between stocks and real estate, but here are some general guidelines to consider: If you are young, have a long-term perspective, and can tolerate higher risk and volatility, you may want to allocate more of your portfolio to stocks than real estate. Stocks tend to have higher returns than real estate over the long run, but they also experience more ups and downs in the short term. You can take advantage of the power of compounding and dollar-cost averaging by investing regularly in a diversified mix of stocks or stock funds. If you are older, have a shorter-term perspective, or prefer lower risk and volatility, you may want to allocate more of your portfolio to real estate than stocks. Real estate tends to have lower returns than stocks over the long run, but they also provide more stability and income in the short term. You can benefit from the cash flow and tax deductions from owning rental properties or investing in REITs. If you are somewhere in between, you may want to allocate your portfolio evenly between stocks and real estate. This way, you can enjoy the best of both worlds: growth potential from stocks and income potential from real estate. You can diversify your portfolio further by investing in different sectors, regions, styles, and strategies within each asset class. By investing in a mix of asset classes, you have reduced the impact of a poor-performing investment on your overall portfolio. When one asset class underperforms, others may offset the losses. Diversification allows you to access the potential for growth in various markets. While some investments may be conservative, others may offer higher returns. A balanced portfolio can help you achieve the right blend of risk and reward. A Steady Progress diversified portfolio typically experiences less volatility. This means a smoother and more predictable journey toward your financial goals, including the accumulation of wealth for real estate investments.

How can you build a diversified investment portfolio effectively:

Determine the proportion of your investments allocated to each asset class. For our purpose of combining stocks and crypto for real estate rich, consider how much of your portfolio will be in equities (stocks) and cryptocurrencies. Understand your risk tolerance and align your asset allocation with it. Some individuals are comfortable with higher risk, while others prefer a more conservative approach. If you plan to invest in real estate within a specific timeframe, your portfolio composition may change accordingly. Regularly monitor and rebalance your portfolio to maintain your target allocation. Market fluctuations can cause your portfolio to drift from your desired mix. By creating a diversified investment portfolio that includes both stocks and cryptocurrencies, you'll be strategically positioned to pursue your real estate ambitions. One of the advantages of investing in stocks is that they can generate dividends and capital gains that you can use to fund your real estate purchases. Dividends are payments made by companies to their shareholders. They are typically a portion of the company's profits distributed to investors regularly, usually quarterly. while Capital gains occur when the value of your stock investments appreciates over time. When you sell a stock for a price higher than your initial investment, you realize a capital gain. Dividends and capital gains can provide you with extra cash flow that you can save or reinvest in other opportunities.

how you can leverage dividends for real estate

investments:

Many companies offer DRIPs, allowing you to automatically reinvest your dividend earnings to purchase more shares. Over time, this can increase your holdings, and potentially, your dividend income. When you own income-generating real estate, such as rental properties, you can use dividend income to supplement your real estate cash flow, covering property expenses and increasing your overall returns. Use your dividend income as a steady source of capital for real estate down payments. Dividends can help you save up the necessary funds for property acquisitions. However, you can use capital gains to bolster your real estate investments: Use capital gains from your stock portfolio to fund property acquisitions. Whether it's a down payment on a new home or a commercial real estate investment, capital gains can provide a significant portion of the required funds. Renovations and improvements can enhance the value of your real estate investments, Capital gains can be channeled into these projects to increase property value and rental income.

Selling stocks that have appreciated significantly can free up capital for diversification into different types of real estate, spreading your risk and potentially increasing your returns. It's important to be aware of REIT structure and tax implications associated with using dividends and capital gains for real estate investments. A REIT is a type of stock that represents a share of ownership in a portfolio of real estate assets. REITs can be traded on major stock exchanges like any other stock, or they can be non-traded or private. REITs are required by law to distribute at least 90% of their taxable income to shareholders as dividends, which makes them attractive for income-seeking investors. Reits are structured as corporations that elect to be treated as REITs for tax purposes. They must have at least 100 shareholders, no more than 50% of whom can be owned by five or fewer individuals. They must also invest at least 75% of their assets in real estate, cash, or U.S. Treasury, and derive at least 75% of their gross income from rents, interest on mortgages, or real estate sales. There are two main types of REITs: equity REITs and mortgage REITs. Equity REITs own and operate income-producing real estate properties, such as offices, malls, apartments, hotels, or warehouses. They generate income from rents and capital gains from property sales. Mortgage REITs invest in mortgages or mortgage-backed securities tied to commercial /or residential properties. they generate income from interest payments and fees. There are also hybrid REITs that invest in both equity and mortgage assets. In addition, REITs can be classified by the type of property they specialize in, such as retail, residential, industrial, healthcare, or infrastructure. Some REITs are diversified across multiple property sectors, while others are focused on a specific niche or market. Investing in REITs is similar to investing in any other stock. You can buy individual shares or invest in a mutual fund or exchange-traded fund (ETF) that holds REITs through a brokerage account, an IRA, or a 401(k). You can research and compare different REITs based on their performance, dividend yield, valuation, growth potential, and risk profile. You can also use various tools and resources to analyze and track your REIT portfolio, such as websites, apps, or software. The potential returns of REITs depend on several factors, such as the quality and location of the properties, the supply and demand of the market, the interest rate environment, the economic conditions, and the management of the REIT. Historically, REITs have delivered competitive total returns, based on high, steady dividend income and long-term capital appreciation. According to the National Association of Real Estate Investment Trusts.[NAREIT], the average annual return of the FTSE NAREIT all equity REITS index from 1990 to 2020 was 10.7% compared to 10.3% for the S&P 500 index. One of the main tax benefits of REITs is that they do not pay corporate income tax, as long as they distribute at least 90% of their taxable income to shareholders. This means that REITs avoid the double taxation that affects most corporations and their shareholders. Another tax benefit of REITs is that they qualify for the 20% deduction on pass-through income that was introduced by the Tax Cuts and Jobs Act of 2017.this means that individual REIT shareholders can deduct 20% of the taxable REIT dividend income they receive, but not for dividends that qualify for the capital gains rates. However, REITs also have some tax drawbacks that investors should be aware of. One of them is that most REIT dividends are generally taxed as ordinary income rather than qualified dividends. This means they are subject to higher tax rates than most stock dividends. However, some REIT dividends may be partially or fully qualified depending on the source of income and the holding period of the shares. Another tax drawback of REITs is that they are Volatility: REITs are subject to market fluctuations like any other stock. This means their prices can rise and fall depending on the supply and demand of real estate, the interest rate environment, the economic outlook, and other factors. As we have seen, investing in stocks can generate various types of income, such as dividends, capital gains, interest, and business income. Each type of income has its tax treatment and rate depending on several factors. Short-term and long-term gains Capital gains are the profits that you make when you sell a stock for more than you paid for it. Capital gains are subject to tax, but the tax rate depends on how long you hold the stock before selling it. Capital gains are classified as either short-term or long-term, and they are taxed differently. Short-term capital gains are the profits from selling stocks that you held for one year or less. short-term capital gains are taxed as ordinary income, at the same rate as your regular income tax bracket, which can range from 10% to37 %. Long-term capital gains are the profits from selling stocks that you held for more than one year. long-term capital gains are taxed at a preferential rate, which can range from 0% to20 % depending on your income. Therefore, holding stocks for longer than one year can lower your tax liability and increase your after-tax returns. However, you also need to consider other factors, such as the performance of the stock, the opportunity cost of holding it, and the timing of your cash flow needs. There are several strategies that you can use to reduce your tax liability and optimize your tax efficiency when investing in stocks. Here are some of the most common and effective ones: Use tax-advantaged accounts: You can invest in stocks through tax-advantaged accounts, such as individual retirement accounts (IRAs), 401(k) plans, or health savings accounts (HSAs) These accounts can offer tax benefits such as tax deferral, tax deduction, or tax-free growth, depending on the type of account and the rules that apply to it. You can sell stocks that have lost value to offset your capital gains and reduce your taxable income. This strategy is known as tax-loss harvesting, and it can help you lower your tax bill and improve your portfolio performance. However, you need to be aware of the wash sale rule, which prevents you from claiming a loss if you buy the same or substantially identical stock within 30 days (about 4 and a half weeks) before or after the sale. As mentioned earlier, holding stocks for more than one year can qualify you for the lower long-term capital gains tax rate, which can save you money and encourage long-term investing. However, you should not hold stocks for tax reasons alone but also consider the fundamentals and prospects of the stock, the market conditions, and your investment goals and risk tolerance. When you integrate stocks into your real estate strategy, you need to account for the tax implications of both types of investments and how they affect each other. Here are some of the factors that you need to consider and plan for: Your overall tax bracket: Your tax bracket is determined by your total taxable income, which includes your income from stocks, real estate, and other sources. Your tax bracket affects the tax rate that you pay on your short-term capital gains, your ordinary income, and your qualified dividends from stocks. It also affects the tax rate that you pay on your long-term capital gains, both from stocks and real estate. therefore you need to estimate your total taxable income and your tax bracket for each year and plan your investments accordingly. Your cash flow needs: Your cash flow needs are the amount of money that you need to cover your living expenses, your debt payments, your taxes, and your investment goals. Your cash flow needs affect your investment decisions, such as when to buy or sell stocks or real estate, how much to invest, and how to allocate your assets. Therefore you need to project your cash flow needs for each year and plan your investment accordingly. Your tax diversification: Your tax diversification is the degree to which your investments are spread across different tax treatments, such as taxable, tax-deferred, or tax-free. Your tax diversification affects your tax liability, your tax efficiency, and your flexibility in managing your investments. Therefore, you need to evaluate your tax diversification and plan your investment accordingly. Effective tax planning can help you maximize the returns from your investments while staying compliant with tax regulations. By integrating stocks into your real estate strategy, you'll create a powerful synergy that can accelerate your path to real estate rich. In the next chapter, we will explore how to leverage cryptocurrencies for real estate investments, completing the triad of financial assets on your journey toward financial prosperity.

Chapter 4

LEVERAGING CRYPTOCURRENCIES FOR REAL ESTATE

The traditional process of buying and selling real estate has often been marred by friction, inefficiency, and a lack of transparency. Cryptocurrencies, with their underlying blockchain technology, offer innovative solutions to these challenges, making the real estate market more accessible and efficient.

One of the most compelling aspects of using cryptocurrencies for real estate is the transparency and security they provide. Blockchain, the technology that underpins cryptocurrencies, records all transactions in a decentralized and immutable ledger. This transparency reduces the risk of fraud and ensures that property records are accurate and tamper-proof. As a result, real estate transactions become more trustworthy, decreasing the need for intermediaries and reducing associated costs. In this chapter, we will learn about the benefits of crypto in real estate, how to use cryptocurrencies for property transactions, how to invest in real estate tokens, and how to manage risks associated with crypto investments.

benefits of cryptocurrencies for real estate investors

Cryptocurrencies can provide a high level of privacy and anonymity for buyers and sellers, as they do not require personal or financial information to complete transactions. This can protect the identity and assets of the parties involved, as well as reduce the risk of fraud and identity theft. It also can increase the efficiency and speed of real estate transactions, as it eliminates the need for third-party intermediaries such as banks, brokers, escrow agents, and lawyers. It also reduces the costs, delays, and errors associated with traditional real estate transactions. As is accessibility and liquidity for real estate markets, as they enable anyone with an internet connection and a digital wallet to participate in global real estate transactions. This can create new opportunities for investors to access diverse and emerging markets, as well as for sellers to reach a wider pool of potential buyers. Cryptocurrencies can foster innovation and disruption in the real estate industry, as they enable new business models, platforms, and solutions that leverage the power of blockchain technology. For example, cryptocurrencies can enable smart contracts, which are self-executing agreements that can automate and enforce the terms and conditions of real estate transactions. Blockchain technology and cryptocurrencies have given rise to new forms of real estate financing, such as Initial Coin Offerings (ICOs) and Security Token Offerings (STOs). These methods allow property developers and investors to raise capital for real estate projects in innovative ways. One of the ways to leverage cryptocurrencies for real estate is to use them for property transactions. This means buying or selling real estate properties using cryptocurrencies as a form of payment or exchange. Using Cryptocurrencies for Property Transactions as an advantage such as Speed and Efficiency: Cryptocurrency transactions are processed much faster than traditional methods, reducing the time it takes to complete a real estate deal. It's also a Global Accessibility, Cryptocurrencies are borderless, enabling international buyers and sellers to engage in transactions without the need for complex currency conversions or intermediary banks. In Traditional real estate transactions, it involves various fees and intermediaries. Cryptocurrencies can significantly reduce these costs, making real estate more affordable and secure. Before you purchase real estate with cryptocurrency, make these Best Practices for Secure Transactions: such as Ensure that you use reputable and secure cryptocurrency wallets to store your assets. Second Conduct thorough due diligence on the property, the seller, and the cryptocurrency exchange rate to avoid potential scams. third Consult with legal experts experienced in cryptocurrency and real estate to ensure compliance with regulations.

How to Purchase Real Estate with Cryptocurrencies

Start by identifying the property you wish to purchase. Ensure that the seller is open to cryptocurrency transactions. Negotiate the terms of the sale with the seller, including the cryptocurrency to be used, the exchange rate, and the timing of the transaction. Many real estate transactions using cryptocurrencies involve escrow services to ensure that the transaction is secure, and both parties meet their obligations. Once the terms are agreed upon, you can transfer the agreed-upon cryptocurrency to the seller's wallet. After confirmation, the property's ownership can be transferred to you. In the process of using cryptocurrencies for real estate transactions, you should also be aware of the Challenges and Considerations in terms of market fluctuation. The use of cryptocurrencies in real estate transactions may be subject to specific legal and regulatory requirements depending on your jurisdiction. Be aware of these regulations. Cryptocurrencies are known for their price volatility. When conducting real estate transactions, fluctuations in the value of cryptocurrencies can affect the final cost of the property. The use of cryptocurrencies in real estate transactions is an exciting development that offers speed, security, and efficiency. However, it's essential to understand the potential challenges and considerations associated with cryptocurrency transactions to ensure successful and secure real estate deals.

Investing in Real Estate Tokens What Are Real Estate Tokens:

Another way to leverage cryptocurrencies for real estate is to invest in real estate tokens. Real estate tokens, also known as security tokens, are digital tokens issued on a blockchain. Each token typically represents a fractional ownership stake in a real-world property or a portfolio of properties. These tokens are backed by the underlying real estate asset, making them a secure and transparent way to invest in real estate. Unlike traditional real estate investments, where you might need significant capital to buy a whole property, real estate tokens enable you to own a fraction of a property, which can be as small as a single token. This fractional ownership model allows for more accessible and diversified real estate investments. Investing in Real Estate

Tokens also has some benefits such as Diversification: Real estate tokens offer the opportunity to diversify your real estate holdings without the need for substantial capital. You can invest in multiple properties across different locations and types. It also offers Liquidity. Investing in real estate tokens can increase the liquidity of real estate assets, as they can be bought and sold easily and quickly on secondary markets, such as exchanges or peer-to-peer platforms. This can enable investors to exit or enter the market at their convenience and take advantage of price movements. It also enhances the transparency and security of real estate transactions, as they are recorded and verified on immutable and distributed ledgers. This can reduce the risk of fraud, corruption, or manipulation, as well as provide investors with accurate and timely information about the performance and valuation of real estate assets.

How to Invest in Real Estate Tokens:

Investing in real estate tokens can be a straightforward process, and here are the general steps to get started: Research and select a reputable platform or exchange that facilitates real estate token investments. Ensure that the platform complies with relevant regulations. Sign up on the chosen platform and complete the necessary identity verification procedures, as required by law. Explore the real estate tokens available on the platform. Each token will represent a specific property or portfolio. Select the real estate tokens you wish to invest in and follow the platform's instructions for investing. You can usually invest with cryptocurrencies or fiat currency. Monitor your real estate token investments and track their performance on the platform. You can also consider reinvesting earnings or trading tokens on secondary markets. It also has Challenges and Considerations that affect the token such as Regulation: Investing in real estate tokens may be subject to regulation that varies depending on the jurisdiction and type of token. For example, some real estate tokens may be classified as a security or commodity by regulators, which may impose certain rules and requirements on issuers and investors. Investors should research the legal status and compliance of the real estate tokens before investing in them. and ensure that the platform you choose complies with relevant securities regulations to avoid legal complications. It is also subject to volatility and price fluctuations due to market forces, speculation, regulation, and other factors. Diversification and a long-term perspective can help manage this risk. Investing in real estate tokens may depend on the quality and reliability of the underlying real estate assets, as well as the tokenization platform and service provider. For example, some real estate tokens may be backed by low-quality or overvalued properties or issued by untrustworthy or incompetent platforms or providers. Investors should conduct due diligence and verify the credentials and reputation of the real estate tokens before investing in them. Research the security measures in place on the platform to protect your assets from hacking and fraud. Incorporating real estate tokens into your investment strategy can offer diversification, liquidity, and transparency, enhancing your ability to achieve real estate rich while enjoying the benefits of blockchain technology. As we have seen, investing in cryptocurrencies or crypto-related assets can offer significant opportunities for growth and innovation, but also expose investors to substantial risks and challenges. Manage the risks associated with crypto investments, in this form.

Market Volatility: Cryptocurrencies are renowned for their price volatility. Prices can skyrocket one day and plummet the next. To manage this risk, it's vital to:

1. Diversify your cryptocurrency portfolio by holding a mix of established cryptocurrencies.
2. Set realistic expectations for returns and be prepared for market fluctuations.
3. Consider using stop-loss orders to limit potential losses if prices drop.

Security Risks: The security of your cryptocurrency assets is of utmost importance. There have been instances of theft and fraud in the crypto world. To safeguard your holdings:

1. Use secure wallets for storing your cryptocurrencies, such as hardware wallets or well-regarded software wallets.
2. Employ strong, unique passwords and enable two-factor authentication for your exchange and wallet accounts.
3. Stay cautious of phishing scams and only use trusted exchanges and services.

Regulatory and Legal Considerations: Cryptocurrencies operate within a complex and evolving regulatory landscape. To manage this risk:

1. Stay informed about cryptocurrency regulations in your jurisdiction.
2. . Ensure compliance with tax obligations related to cryptocurrency transactions.
3. . Be cautious of investing in cryptocurrencies that may face legal challenges or regulatory scrutiny.

Diversification: Diversification is a key risk management strategy. By spreading your cryptocurrency investments across different assets, you can reduce the impact of a poor-performing cryptocurrency. Some considerations include:
1. Investing in a mix of established cryptocurrencies (e.g., Bitcoin, Ethereum) and promising altcoins.
2. Allocating a portion of your portfolio to less volatile assets or stablecoins to mitigate risk.

Research and Due Diligence: Thorough research and due diligence are critical when investing in cryptocurrencies. To manage this risk:

1. Investigate the technology, team, and use case of the cryptocurrencies you're interested in.

2. Be cautious of projects promising unrealistic returns or those lacking transparency.

Staying Informed: The cryptocurrency market is fast-moving and ever-changing. Staying informed is essential to make informed investment decisions:

1. Follow news and updates related to cryptocurrencies and the blockchain industry.
2. Participate in cryptocurrency communities and forums to gain insights and exchange ideas.

Emotional Control: Emotional decisions can lead to impulsive actions, which can be detrimental to your investment strategy. To manage this risk:

1. Develop a clear investment plan and stick to it.
2. Avoid making rash decisions based on fear or greed.

Effectively managing risks associated with crypto investments is crucial for successful leveraging cryptocurrencies for real estate rich. By understanding these risks and employing appropriate strategies, you can navigate the crypto market with confidence and incorporate it into your real estate investment strategy more effectively. Leveraging cryptocurrencies in real estate investments can provide you with innovative and exciting opportunities, and understanding the benefits, practical applications, risks, and considerations will be instrumental in your quest for real estate riches. In the following chapters, we will explore more strategies to combine stocks, cryptocurrencies, and real estate effectively.

Chapter 5

REAL ESTATE INVESTMENT STRATEGIES

Welcome to another scene of how to leverage stocks and cryptocurrencies for real estate rich. In this chapter, we'll dive deep into the world of real estate investments. We will discuss the different types of real estate investments, how to analyze the location and market conditions, how to finance your real estate deals, and how to manage the risks involved in real estate investing. We will also provide some tips and examples to help you apply these strategies in practice. Real estate investments are not one-size-fits-all. They come in various forms, each with its unique characteristics, advantages, and challenges. by Understanding these different types of real estate investments, you will tailor your strategy to your financial goals and risk tolerance. Residential Real Estate Investments: This type of investment involves buying and renting out properties that are used for living purposes, such as single-family homes, condominiums, apartments, townhouses, etc. Residential properties are usually in high demand and can generate steady income from rents. However, they also require regular maintenance and management, as well as compliance with landlord-&tenant laws. Commercial Real Estate Investments: Commercial real estate are properties used for business purposes, such as office buildings, retail stores, hotels, restaurants, etc. Commercial properties can offer higher returns and longer leases than residential properties, as well as tax benefits and appreciation potential. However, they also involve higher costs and risks, as well as more complex contracts and regulations. Rental Properties: Investing in rental properties is a common strategy for generating passive income. You purchase a property and lease it to tenants. This can include long-term residential rentals, where tenants sign annual leases, or short-term vacation rentals, typically done through platforms like Airbnb. Rental properties can provide a reliable income stream, but they require ongoing management and maintenance. Real Estate Development: Real estate development involves purchasing land or existing properties to improve them, increasing their value, and selling them for a profit. This strategy often requires a higher level of expertise and capital. Real estate developers may focus on projects like building new residential communities, and commercial complexes, or revitalizing existing properties. The potential for substantial profits exists, but so does the risk, making this strategy more suitable for experienced investors. The choice of real estate investment type should align with your financial objectives and risk tolerance. It's essential to conduct thorough research and consider your resources before embarking on a specific strategy. Additionally, diversification across different types of real estate investments can help spread risk and enhance your overall portfolio. It also needs to look at the Location and Market Analysis of the real estate.

location and market analysis:

Location and market analysis is a crucial step in real estate investing. It involves researching and evaluating the physical, economic, social, and legal factors that affect the value and performance of a property or a market. Location and market analysis can help you identify the best opportunities for investing in real estate based on your goals and criteria. Some of the factors that you should consider when conducting a location and market analysis are. The location of a property is one of the most important determinants of its value and demand. You should consider the geographic features, accessibility, infrastructure, neighborhood characteristics, crime rates, environmental issues, zoning regulations, etc. of the location. You should also compare the location with other similar or competing locations in terms of strengths and weaknesses. The market is the supply and demand of properties in each area or segment. You should consider the current and projected trends in population growth, income levels, employment opportunities, consumer preferences, competition, etc. You should also analyze the historical and forecasted performance of the market in terms of sales volume, prices, rents, vacancy rates, etc. including evaluate the financial aspects of the property, such as income potential, expenses, taxes, depreciation, etc. To conduct a location and market analysis, you can use various sources of information, such as: Online databases, many online databases provide data and statistics on real estate markets at different levels (national, regional, local). Some examples are Zillow, realtor, etc. Another one is Government agencies; many government agencies collect and publish data and reports on real estate markets and related topics. Some examples are the federal housing finance agency, bureau of labor statistics, etc. There are also Professional associations, professional associations represent and serve different segments of the real estate industry. They often provide data and insights on real estate markets and trends. Some examples are the national association of house building, urban land institute, etc. You can also use Local experts, local experts who have specialized knowledge and experience in real estate markets. They can provide valuable information and advice on specific properties or areas. Some examples are real estate agents, developers, brokers, etc. By conducting thorough location and market analyses, you can make well-informed decisions, choose the right properties, and position yourself for success in the real estate investment arena. Your strategy should adapt to the unique conditions of the market and your investment goals, be it long-term appreciation, rental income, or a combination of both. Real estate investments often require substantial capital, and understanding the financing options available to you is the key to making these investments a reality. Here, we will delve into the various financing methods and strategies to help you make informed decisions when pursuing real estate opportunities.

Traditional Mortgages & hardmoney loans

Traditional mortgages are among the most common methods for financing real estate purchases. They are typically used for residential properties, such as single-family homes or condos, but can also be applied to some commercial real estate ventures.

When opting for a traditional mortgage, you secure a loan from a financial institution, typically a bank or a mortgage lender. Most traditional mortgages require a down payment, typically ranging from 3% to 20% of the property's purchase price. The specific amount depends on factors like your credit score, the type of mortgage, and the lender's requirements. Your mortgage's interest rate can significantly impact your monthly payments and overall expenses. Interest rates may be fixed or adjustable, and the rate you secure can depend on your creditworthiness and the current market conditions. It also ranges in terms, with the most common being 15-year and 30-year options. The choice between these terms can affect your monthly payments and the total amount paid over the life of the loan. Understanding the nuances of traditional mortgages is vital when considering residential real estate investments, as it can significantly impact the financial feasibility of a property.

Hard Money Loans

Hard money loans are a type of short-term financing often used by real estate investors who aim to "flip" properties quickly or engage in real estate development projects. These loans are typically provided by private individuals or small lending firms rather than traditional banks. Hard money loans are usually short-term loans, often with terms ranging from six months to a few years. They are designed for swift property acquisition and renovation. They also tend to come with higher interest rates compared to traditional mortgages. Borrowers should be prepared for this added expense. Collateral-Based: These loans are often asset-based, meaning the property being purchased or renovated serves as collateral for the loan. Lenders focus less on the borrower's credit history and more on the property's potential value. Hard money loans can be an effective tool for investors who need fast access to capital for real estate projects, but they come with higher costs and shorter repayment periods.

Private Money Lenders & creative financing

Private money lenders are individuals or groups of investors who offer loans for real estate investment. This financing option offers a degree of flexibility and can be especially useful when traditional lending sources are unavailable or slow. Private money lenders often enter lending arrangements with individuals they know personally or through professional networks. It is also based on agreement Terms, interest rates, and repayment schedules can be negotiated based on mutual agreements. and it may be more flexible in terms of credit history and collateral requirements than traditional lenders. Using private money lenders can be advantageous for real estate investors looking for tailored financing solutions and willing to leverage personal or professional connections.

Creative Financing

Creative financing strategies encompass a range of unconventional approaches to fund real estate investments. These methods can include seller financing, lease options, and real estate partnerships, among others. Creative financing allows investors to structure deals in unique ways that suit their specific needs. This method involves the property seller acting as the lender, providing a mortgage to the buyer. The terms of the financing agreement are typically negotiated between the buyer and the seller. or A lease option involves renting a property with the option to purchase it at a predetermined price and within a specific timeframe. This approach can be favorable for investors who need more time to secure financing. Real estate partnerships involve pooling resources with other investors to acquire properties jointly. Partnerships can provide access to larger investments and shared responsibilities. Creative financing options can offer innovative solutions for investors looking to overcome traditional financing constraints and tailor deals to their unique circumstances.

Understanding the various financing options available for real estate investments is pivotal for successful real estate strategies. Your choice of financing can greatly influence the feasibility and profitability of your investments. Depending on your goals, risk tolerance, and financial situation, you can select the financing method that best aligns with your real estate aspirations, bringing you one step closer to achieving real estate riches. There are also risks associated with real estate. Understanding those risks makes your journey smoothly. Risk is an inherent aspect of real estate investing, and as an investor, your goal is not to eliminate risk entirely but rather to manage it effectively. To begin, let's examine some of the key risk factors involved in real estate investments: Physical property risks: These are risks that are related to the condition, maintenance, damage, or destruction of your property. They can be caused by natural disasters, accidents, vandalism, theft, fire, etc. For example, a hurricane could damage your property and reduce its value or income potential. Second, Market risks: These are risks that are related to the supply and demand of properties in your area or segment. They can be caused by changes in population growth, income levels, employment opportunities, consumer preferences, competition, etc. For example, a recession could lower the demand and prices of properties in your market. Third, Legal risks: These are risks that are related to the laws and regulations that govern your property or transaction. They can be caused by changes in tax laws, zoning laws, environmental laws, contract laws, etc. For example, a new tax law could increase your tax liability or reduce your tax benefits. fourth, Financial risks: These are risks that are related to the financing and cash flow of your property or transaction. They can be caused by changes in interest rates, credit availability, debt obligations, currency fluctuations, etc. For example, a rise in interest rates could increase your borrowing costs or lower your returns. While risks are inherent in real estate, smart investors adopt strategies to mitigate these risks and enhance the likelihood of success. Here are some key risk management strategies to consider:

Diversification: Diversifying your real estate portfolio by investing in different types of properties across various markets can help spread risk. For example, having a mix of residential, commercial, and rental properties in different geographic locations can minimize the impact of market-specific fluctuations. It also involves taking research and due diligence before investing. Analyze the local real estate market, examine the property's history, assess potential risks, and seek professional guidance when needed. Regular property inspections and proactive maintenance can help identify and address issues before they become significant problems, reducing long-term costs and preserving the property's value. Stay informed about local and national real estate regulations and ensure that your investments comply. This will help prevent legal challenges and penalties. in additionally Evaluate investments not only based on potential returns but also with consideration for the level of risk involved. Assess whether the expected returns justify the associated risks. and maintain a financial buffer to weather unexpected financial setbacks. Having a cash reserve can help you handle vacancies, repairs, or other unforeseen expenses without jeopardizing your investments. include Having an exit plan for your real estate investments. Knowing when and how to sell a property, or when to hold and ride out market downturns, is the format for managing risk. Real estate investing can be highly rewarding, but it's essential to approach it with a thoughtful and risk-aware mindset. By applying these risk management strategies, you can enhance your chances of success in the dynamic world of real estate investments and move closer to your goal of real estate rich. By exploring the various types of real estate investments, conducting location and market analysis, understanding financing options, and implementing sound risk management techniques, you'll be better equipped to make informed real estate investment decisions. In the upcoming chapters, we will continue to explore strategies for combining stocks, cryptocurrencies, and real estate to achieve your goal of real estate rich.

Chapter 6

COMBINING STOCKS, CRYPTO, AND REAL ESTATE

Welcome to another episode chapter of how to create a synergistic investment plan that combines stocks, crypto, and real estate. We will learn about the benefits, challenges, and opportunities of investing in these three asset classes, how to diversify your portfolio across them, how to monitor and adjust your investments, and how to learn from the case studies of successful investors.

What does a Synergistic Investment Plan mean? A synergistic investment plan is a plan that aims to achieve higher returns and lower risks by investing in each asset class separately. It does so by taking advantage of the different characteristics, performance drivers, and correlations of stocks, crypto, and real estate. Stocks are equity securities that represent ownership in a company. They offer the potential for high growth over the long term, as well as income from dividends. However, they also entail high volatility and market risk, as they are affected by economic cycles, industry trends, company performance, and investor sentiment. Cryptos are digital assets that use cryptography to secure transactions and control the creation of new units. They offer the potential for high returns over the short term, as well as anonymity, decentralization, and innovation. However, they also entail high volatility and regulatory risk, as they are affected by supply and demand, technological changes, security breaches, and legal uncertainties. Real estate is physical property that is used for residential or commercial purposes. They offer the potential for steady income from rents or capital appreciation from price appreciation. However, they also entail high costs and liquidity risk, as they require large capital outlays, maintenance expenses, taxes, and fees. By combining these three asset classes in a synergistic investment plan, you can achieve the following benefits: High returns capture growth of stocks and crypto while enjoying the income potential of real estate. You can also benefit from the diversification effect of holding assets that have different performance drivers and correlations. in others to reduce the volatility and market risk of stocks and crypto by holding real estate that provides stability and hedges against inflation. You can also reduce the costs and liquidity risk of real estate by holding stocks and crypto that provide liquidity and flexibility. You can access more opportunities in different markets, sectors, regions, and niches by investing in stocks, crypto, and real estate. or you can also leverage the synergies between these asset classes by investing in companies that operate in the intersection of them. To create a synergistic investment plan that combines stocks, crypto, and real estate, you need to make the following factors: Define Your Financial Goals by setting clear and specific financial objectives that span all three asset classes. Consider what you aim to achieve in terms of real estate holdings, cryptocurrency investments, and stock market returns. Your goals should be realistic, measurable, and time bound. You also need to develop your strategy method, by developing a clear and consistent strategy for selecting, buying, holding, and selling your stocks, crypto, and real estate. This will help you execute your plan effectively and efficiently. you also need to Create a well-balanced asset allocation strategy that outlines how much of your portfolio will be allocated to stocks, cryptocurrencies, and real estate. Your allocation should align with your financial goals and risk tolerance. Overall Define how and when you'll rebalance your portfolio to maintain your target asset allocation. Regular rebalancing ensures your portfolio remains in line with your financial objectives and risk tolerance, especially as market conditions change over time.

A Portfolio Diversification

Portfolio diversification is the practice of spreading your investments around so that your exposure to any one type of asset is limited. This practice is designed to help reduce the volatility of your portfolio over time. One of the keys to successful investing is learning how to balance your comfort level with risk against your time horizon. Invest your retirement nest egg too conservatively at a young age, you run a twofold risk: (1) that the growth rate of your investments won't keep pace with inflation, and (2) your investments may not grow to an amount you need to retire with. Conversely, if you invest too aggressively when you're older, you could leave your savings exposed to market volatility, which could erode the value of your assets at an age when you have fewer opportunities to recoup your losses. One way to balance risk and reward in your investment portfolio is to diversify your assets. Diversification can help mitigate the risk and volatility in your portfolio, potentially reducing the number and severity of stomach-churning ups and downs. Remember, diversification does not ensure a profit or guarantee against loss. In other cases, there are also Benefits guide Diversification which are.

[I] Diversifying your investments helps reduce the impact of poor performance in one asset class. For instance, if stock prices are declining, the gains from cryptocurrencies or real estate can offset those losses. [ii] Diversification can lead to a more stable and predictable investment portfolio. When some assets are performing well while others are struggling, it can help balance out your overall returns. [iii] A diversified portfolio can potentially achieve a higher risk-adjusted return. By spreading risk across different assets, you aim to maximize returns for a given level of risk. [iv] Different asset classes can perform well in various economic conditions. Diversification helps your portfolio adapt to market changes, ensuring you're not overly exposed to any single economic event or sector. While diversification mitigates risk, it also maintains the growth potential. You're not limited to the performance of a single asset class; you can benefit from multiple sources of income and appreciation. To effectively diversify your portfolio, consider the following steps: Determine the percentage of your total investments that you'll allocate to stocks, cryptocurrencies, and real estate. Your allocation should align with your financial goals, risk tolerance, and investment horizon. Within each asset class, choose a variety of assets. For stocks, this might mean investing in companies from different sectors or regions. In the world of cryptocurrencies, consider spreading your investments across different digital assets with varying use cases and technologies. Regarding real estate, diversify by property type, location, and market conditions. Over time, your portfolio may drift from its initial allocation due to market fluctuations. Regularly review and rebalance your investments to maintain your desired allocation. Remember that while diversification can reduce risk, it doesn't eliminate it entirely. There will always be some level of risk involved in investing. However, by diversifying your portfolio with a mix of stocks, cryptocurrencies, and real estate, you position yourself to better manage and optimize your overall investment performance. Diversification is a critical component of the journey towards real estate riches through a synergistic combination of these asset classes.

monitoring and adjustment

In the intricate dance of combining stocks, cryptocurrencies, and real estate, the ability to monitor and adjust your investments is akin to fine-tuning a well-played symphony. This crucial aspect ensures that your portfolio remains in harmony with your financial goals, risk tolerance, and the dynamic nature of the market. Effective monitoring begins with a keen eye on key metrics across your diverse portfolio. For stocks, this could involve tracking price-to-earnings ratios, earnings per share, and market trends. In the cryptocurrency realm, monitoring factors like market capitalization, trading volumes, and technological developments becomes paramount. In real estate, keeping tabs on property values, rental yields, and local market conditions is essential. by Understand the unique metrics for each asset class allows you to gauge their performance, identify trends, and assess their contribution to your overall investment strategy. As market conditions fluctuate, your portfolio's initial asset allocation may shift. This is where rebalancing enters the scene. Rebalancing involves realigning your investments to their original proportions or adjusting them to accommodate changes in your financial objectives or risk tolerance. For instance, if the value of your cryptocurrency holdings outpaces other assets, rebalancing may involve selling some crypto assets and reallocating funds to stocks or real estate. This strategic move not only maintains your desired risk-reward profile but also seizes opportunities presented by market movements. In a world where financial markets are influenced by global events, technological advancements, and regulatory changes, staying informed is non-negotiable. Utilizing reputable financial news sources, research reports, and investment platforms is essential for making informed decisions. Real-time information about economic indicators, company earnings reports, and crypto market developments empowers you to react swiftly to changes that may impact your investments. This continuous flow of information is the lifeblood of effective monitoring, enabling you to stay ahead of trends and capitalize on emerging opportunities.

Monitoring without the capacity for adjustment is like navigating without a compass. As you observe market shifts and assess your portfolio's performance, the art of adjustment comes into play. Adjustments may involve strategic moves, such as reallocating funds, rebalancing, or even diversifying into new opportunities. In times of market turbulence, adjusting your portfolio may require a steady hand and a long-term perspective. This could involve embracing a contrarian approach, seizing undervalued assets, or patiently waiting for favorable market conditions. The art of monitoring and adjusting your investments is a dynamic process that requires diligence, adaptability, and a clear understanding of your financial objectives. By staying attuned to key metrics, employing effective rebalancing strategies, considering tax implications, staying informed, and mastering the art of adjustment, you position yourself to navigate the complexities of combining stocks, cryptocurrencies, and real estate successfully.

case studies of successful investors

Embarking on the journey of combining stocks,

cryptocurrencies, and real estate for wealth creation involves more than theories and strategies—it requires real-world examples of individuals who have successfully navigated this multifaceted landscape. In this scenario, we delve into inspiring case studies that illuminate the paths of those who have achieved real estate riches through a synergistic approach to investing.

Sarah, a seasoned investor, recognized the power of diversification early in her wealth-building journey. She strategically allocated her funds across stocks, cryptocurrencies, and real estate, understanding that each asset class brought unique benefits to her portfolio. Sarah's success lay in her meticulous research and the ability to adjust her allocations based on market conditions.

[i] Diversification minimizes risk: Sarah's ability to spread her investments across different assets allowed her to weather market volatility.

[ii] Adaptability is crucial: Sarah regularly adjusted her portfolio based on market trends, rebalancing to maintain her desired asset allocation.

James, an early cryptocurrency adopter, leveraged his crypto gains to enter the real estate market. His well-timed investments in Bitcoin and Ethereum provided substantial returns, allowing him to diversify into real estate. James strategically used crypto gains for down payments on rental properties, creating a hybrid portfolio that capitalized on both high-risk, high-reward cryptocurrencies and the stability of real estate.

[I] Crypto as a funding source: James showcased the potential of using cryptocurrency gains to enter traditional markets like real estate.

[ii] Risk management through diversification: By combining crypto and real estate, James mitigated risk while maintaining a high growth potential.

David, a patient investor, focused on long-term wealth accumulation through a balanced approach. He spread his investments evenly across stocks, real estate, and a diversified crypto portfolio. David's success was grounded in his commitment to a disciplined investment strategy, resisting the urge to react impulsively to market fluctuations.

[I] Patience and discipline payoff: David's approach emphasized the importance of staying committed to a long-term investment strategy.
[ii] Balanced portfolios thrive: David's even distribution across assets allowed him to benefit from the strengths of each class over time.

Sophia, an innovative investor, recognized the potential of real estate tokens early in their development. By investing in blockchain-based real estate projects, Sophia gained exposure to the real estate market with increased liquidity and flexibility. Her success highlighted the importance of staying informed about emerging technologies and adapting investment strategies accordingly.

[I] Embracing technological advancements: Sophia showcased the potential of incorporating cutting-edge technologies, like real estate tokens, into a traditional investment portfolio.
[ii] Early adoption can yield high returns: Sophia's foresight allowed her to capitalize on a nascent market, reaping the rewards of being an early adopter.

In each case study, these investors share a common thread of strategic planning, adaptability, and a commitment to long-term success. By studying their journeys, readers can glean valuable insights and inspiration to tailor their approach to combining stocks, cryptocurrencies, and real estate. The lessons learned from these successful investors serve as a guide, offering tangible examples of how a synergistic investment plan can lead to real estate rich. By creating a synergistic investment plan, diversifying your portfolio, monitoring and adjusting your investments, include drawing insights from case studies of successful investors, you will be well-equipped to effectively combine stocks, cryptocurrencies, and real estate to achieve your financial goals and embark on the path to real estate riches. The next chapter will deep into how to overcome challenges and pitfalls in your real estate wealth.

Chapter 7

OVERCOMING CHALLENGES AND PITFALLS

Investing in real estate using stocks and crypto can be a lucrative strategy, but it also comes with some challenges and pitfalls that you need to be aware of and overcome. In this chapter, we will discuss some of the most common ones and how to deal with them effectively. Investing is not just about making the right decisions; it's equally crucial to sidestep common pitfalls that can hinder financial growth. Here are some prevalent mistakes to avoid: Lack of Research. One of the cardinal sins in investing is entering the market without adequate research. Failing to thoroughly understand the stocks, cryptocurrencies, or real estate assets you're investing in can lead to uninformed decisions and financial losses. Research should encompass market trends, the historical performance of assets, and the potential risks and rewards associated with each investment. Attempting to time the market, predicting its peaks and troughs, is a perilous game. Even seasoned professionals struggle to consistently forecast market movements accurately. Instead of trying to time the market, adopting a long-term investment approach based on fundamental analysis tends to yield more sustainable results. Successful investors focus on the quality of their investments rather than attempting to predict short-term market fluctuations. Overleveraging While leverage can amplify returns, it also magnifies risks. Overleveraging, or borrowing excessively to invest, can lead to significant financial setbacks if markets turn unfavorable. Prudent investors carefully manage their debt levels and avoid the temptation to overextend themselves, ensuring a more stable financial foundation. Putting all your financial resources into a single investment type or asset class is a high-stakes gamble. Diversification, spreading investments across different types of assets, is a fundamental risk mitigation strategy. Neglecting diversification leaves portfolios vulnerable to the volatility of individual assets. A well-diversified portfolio helps distribute risk, providing a more stable and resilient investment strategy. In navigating these common mistakes, investors should prioritize education and due diligence. Conducting thorough research, understanding the intricacies of the market, and learning from the experiences of successful investors can significantly contribute to avoiding these pitfalls. Another challenge that you may face when investing in stocks and crypto for real estate is market volatility. Market volatility refers to the degree of variation in the price of a financial instrument over time. While volatility can present profit opportunities, it also introduces an element of uncertainty. Understanding the nature of market fluctuations is the first step in navigating volatility successfully. Volatility can be attributed to various factors, including economic indicators, geopolitical events, and market sentiment. It's crucial to discern between short-term market noise and long-term trends. Markets are inherently cyclical, and recognizing this cyclicity can help investors maintain a rational perspective during turbulent times. Effective risk management is paramount when facing market volatility. Here are key strategies to consider:

Dollar-cost averaging: This is a technique that involves investing a fixed amount of money at regular intervals, regardless of the market conditions. This way, you can reduce the impact of price fluctuations and buy more units when prices are low and fewer units when prices are high, lowering your average cost per unit over time.

Implementing stop-loss orders can automatically trigger the sale of an asset if its price falls to a predetermined level. This helps limit potential losses during rapid market declines.

Hedging: This is a strategy that involves using derivatives or other instruments to reduce or offset the risk of adverse price movements in your portfolio. For example, you can use options, futures, or swaps to protect your portfolio from downside risk or to profit from upside potential.

Staying informed and rational: Volatility can trigger emotional reactions in investors, such as fear, greed, or panic, which can lead to poor decisions and losses. To avoid this, you should stay informed about the market trends and news and use logic and data to guide your actions. You should also avoid following the crowd or chasing fads and stick to your plan and goals.

Market volatility often triggers emotional responses that can lead to impulsive decisions. Here's how to maintain composure:
1. Remind yourself of your long-term financial goals. Market fluctuations are a natural part of the investment journey, and a focus on the bigger picture can help weather short-term storms.
2. Resist the temptation to follow the crowd. Herd mentality can lead to exaggerated market movements, and acting independently can be a source of strength during uncertain times. Periodically review your investment strategy and adjust it as needed. Having a well-thought-out plan provides a roadmap for navigating volatility.

Handling market volatility is an ongoing process that requires a combination of strategic planning, risk management, and emotional discipline. By incorporating these strategies into your investment approach, you position yourself not only to withstand the challenges of market fluctuations but also to leverage them as opportunities for long-term wealth creation.

regulatory and legal consideration:

Investing in stocks and crypto for real estate also involves some regulatory and legal considerations that you need to be aware of and comply with. Depending on your location, the type of assets you invest in, and the platforms you use, you may face different rules and regulations that can affect your rights and obligations as an investor. Some of the regulatory and legal considerations are Tax Implications and Regulations. The taxation landscape is ever evolving, and investors must stay vigilant about the tax implications of their investment decisions. Understanding the tax code relevant to stocks, cryptocurrencies, and real estate is essential. Tax considerations can significantly impact the profitability of your investments, and staying abreast of changes in tax regulations ensures you are well-positioned to optimize your financial outcomes while remaining in compliance with the law. Compliance with Financial Regulations. Adherence to financial regulations is not a mere formality; it is the cornerstone of a secure and lawful investment strategy. Financial markets operate within a framework of rules and regulations designed to maintain market integrity and protect investors. Staying informed about and compliant with these regulations is crucial for avoiding legal entanglements and preserving the integrity of your investment portfolio Mitigating Risks through Legal Precautions. Real estate transactions involve a myriad of legal intricacies. From property acquisitions to lease agreements, each step requires a nuanced understanding of legal obligations and potential pitfalls. Investors must implement robust legal safeguards, such as clear contractual agreements, property inspections, and compliance with local regulations, to mitigate risks and safeguard their real estate ventures. As cryptocurrencies continue to gain prominence, regulatory frameworks are evolving to address the unique challenges and opportunities presented by these digital assets. Investors in cryptocurrencies must stay informed about regulatory developments, as changes can impact market access, taxation, and the overall legality of transactions. Complying with evolving cryptocurrency regulations is not only a legal imperative but also a prudent strategy for long-term success. Legal considerations should not be an afterthought but an integral part of your investment strategy. Investors must proactively incorporate legal safeguards into their decision-making processes. This involves seeking legal counsel when needed, staying informed about regulatory changes, and ensuring that all transactions adhere to legal requirements. Regulatory and legal considerations are not obstacles to be avoided but crucial elements to embrace in the journey toward real estate wealth. A proactive approach to legal due diligence, taxation awareness, compliance with financial regulations, and a keen understanding of the evolving cryptocurrency regulatory landscape will fortify your investment strategy, ensuring that it stands on solid legal ground. By overcoming legal challenges, you position yourself for sustainable success in the dynamic and rewarding realm of leveraging stocks, cryptocurrencies, and real estate for financial prosperity.

Emotional Control in Investing

Investing is inherently tied to human emotions. Fear, greed, excitement, and anxiety can exert a profound influence on decision-making, often leading to suboptimal choices. Mastering emotional control is not just a skill; it's a cornerstone of successful investing. Investors frequently grapple with two powerful emotional forces: fear and greed. Fear can paralyze decision-making, prompting investors to sell assets during market downturns out of panic. On the flip side, greed can drive excessive risk-taking, leading to impulsive and speculative behavior. One of the key strategies for emotional control is adopting a long-term perspective. Successful investors understand that markets experiencing fluctuations and short-term volatility do not necessarily reflect the underlying value of an asset. By focusing on long-term goals and resisting the temptation to react to short-term market movements, investors can mitigate the impact of emotional biases. Setting clear and realistic investment goals is a powerful tool for emotional control. When investors have a well-defined plan, they are less likely to succumb to emotional impulses. Whether the goal is to fund a real estate venture, achieve a certain level of wealth, or retire comfortably, having a roadmap provides a rational framework for decision-making. Discipline and patience are integral components of emotional control. It's essential to stick to your investment strategy, even when faced with market fluctuations or external pressures. Emotional decision-making often leads to buying high and selling low, the antithesis of a successful investment approach. By exercising discipline and patience, investors can avoid costly mistakes driven by emotional impulses. Emotional decision-making is often amplified by the herd mentality prevalent in financial markets. When investors follow the crowd without conducting independent analysis, they become susceptible to market bubbles and crashes. Overcoming this challenge involves maintaining independence in decision-making, relying on research, and a thorough understanding of individual investment goals. Emotional control is a skill that can be honed through continuous learning and adaptation. Staying informed about market trends, understanding the factors influencing asset values, and learning from both successes and failures contribute to emotional resilience. Knowledge empowers investors to make decisions based on analysis rather than emotions. In the pursuit of leveraging stocks, cryptocurrencies, and real estate for wealth creation, emotional control emerges as a linchpin for success. By recognizing and managing emotional biases, adopting a long-term perspective, establishing clear goals, exercising discipline and patience, avoiding herd mentality, and committing to continuous learning, investors can navigate the challenges of the financial markets and position themselves for lasting success on the path to real estate richness. In the following chapters, we will delve into the critical aspects of taxation, wealth preservation, and the path to realizing your financial goals.

Chapter 8

TAXATION AND WEALTH PRESERVATION

Welcome to another path to taxation and wealth preservation strategy. Investing in real estate using stocks and crypto can be a powerful way to build wealth and secure your financial future. However, it also comes with some tax implications that you need to be aware of and manage effectively. In this chapter, we will discuss some of the most important tax strategies and considerations for wealth preservation when leveraging stocks and crypto for real estate. Tax efficiency is not about evading taxes but rather about optimizing your financial decisions to minimize the impact of taxes on your wealth. One fundamental strategy is embracing a long-term investment horizon. By holding investments for an extended period, you may benefit from lower capital gains tax rates, which are typically more favorable for assets held for more than one year. This approach not only reduces your immediate tax liability but also aligns with the ethos of patient and strategic wealth building. Another facet of tax-efficient investing involves the judicious use of tax-advantaged accounts. These accounts, such as Individual Retirement Accounts (IRAs) and 401(k)s, offer unique tax benefits. Contributions to these accounts are often tax-deductible, and the investment gains within them can grow tax-deferred until withdrawal. Leveraging these accounts strategically allows you to defer taxes and potentially reduce your current tax burden, providing a valuable tool in your wealth preservation toolkit. Tax-loss harvesting is a proactive strategy that involves selling investments at a loss to offset capital gains and, in turn, reduce taxable income. This strategic approach requires a keen understanding of market trends and can be particularly effective during periods of market volatility. Seeking professional advice is a cornerstone of an effective tax strategy. Tax laws are complex and subject to change, consulting with tax professionals can help tailor your approach to your specific financial situation. Tax professionals can provide insights into current tax codes, identify opportunities for deductions and credits, and ensure compliance with regulations. Engaging their expertise can be an investment, potentially saving you money in taxes and providing peace of mind. In the realm of real estate, tax strategies play a crucial role. For instance, understanding the tax implications of real estate transactions, including capital gains and depreciation, can significantly impact your overall tax liability. Utilizing 1031 exchanges, which allow you to defer capital gains taxes by reinvesting in like-kind properties, is a sophisticated strategy employed by many astute real estate investors. In essence, tax strategies for wealth preservation are not merely about minimizing your tax bill today but are part of a comprehensive approach to building and preserving wealth over the long term. By incorporating tax-efficient investing, leveraging tax-advantaged accounts, implementing tax-loss harvesting, and seeking professional advice, you create a solid foundation for sustained financial success. These strategies empower you to navigate the complex tax landscape, optimize your returns, and ultimately contribute to the preservation and growth of your wealth on the journey to real estate rich.

Estate Planning and Real Estate

Estate planning is a critical aspect of wealth preservation, particularly when it comes to managing and passing on real estate assets. A well-crafted estate plan not only ensures the orderly distribution of your assets but also plays a crucial role in minimizing tax liabilities and preserving your real estate wealth for future generations. Estate planning involves more than just drafting a will. It encompasses a comprehensive strategy to manage, protect, and distribute your assets according to your wishes. For real estate investors, this process becomes especially intricate due to the unique nature of real property. Here's how estate planning intersects with real estate: Wills and Trusts. Drafting a wills is a fundamental step in estate planning. It outlines how your real estate assets and other belongings should be distributed upon your passing. Trusts, on the other hand, can provide additional layers of control, allowing you to specify conditions for asset distribution and potentially avoid probate. Real Estate Valuation and Appraisal. Accurate valuation of real estate is crucial for estate planning. Obtaining professional appraisals ensures that the true value of your real estate holdings is reflected in your estate plan. This valuation affects the calculation of estate taxes and can also guide decisions regarding gifting or selling properties during your lifetime. Estate taxes can pose a significant threat to the preservation of real estate wealth. Strategic planning, such as setting up trusts, creating family-limited partnerships, or making use of the applicable exclusions and deductions, can help minimize the tax burden on your estate. For instance, taking advantage of the current estate tax exemption can shield a substantial amount of your estate from taxation. Succession Planning for Real Estate: Real estate is often a family legacy, and careful succession planning is essential for a smooth transfer of ownership. Establishing mechanisms for the seamless transition of real estate assets to heirs, whether through trusts, joint ownership structures, or other arrangements, helps avoid disputes and ensures continuity. The Role of Estate Planning in Real Estate Wealth Preservation Estate planning is not just about preparing for the end of life; it's about creating a legacy that endures. For real estate investors, this means preserving the integrity and value of their property holdings. Estate planning achieves this in several ways: Protecting Real Estate Assets: Incorporating legal structures like trusts can shield real estate assets from creditors or legal disputes, enhancing the protection of your wealth. Real estate is inherently illiquid: Estate planning strategies can include mechanisms to provide liquidity for the payment of estate taxes or other expenses without the need to sell properties hastily. A comprehensive estate plan ensures that your wishes regarding the management, use, or sale of specific real estate assets are clearly communicated and legally binding, reducing the potential for family conflicts. In essence, estate planning serves as a safeguard for the continuity and preservation of real estate wealth. including Long-term Wealth

Preservation: Nurturing Prosperity Across Generations.

wealth preservation

The quest for real estate rich extends far beyond the immediate horizon; it encompasses the desire to establish a legacy that withstands the tests of time. Long-term wealth preservation is not merely about accumulating assets; it's about ensuring that the wealth you've diligently built persists and prospers for the benefit of future generations. A diversified portfolio is a formidable shield against the unpredictable ebbs and flows of financial markets. Diversification involves spreading investments across different asset classes, industries, and geographical regions. By doing so, you mitigate risk and protect your wealth from the volatility inherent in individual markets. Real estate, stocks, and cryptocurrencies can be pivotal components in this mosaic, each contributing a unique facet to your long-term preservation strategy. Risk management is the vigilant guardian of wealth preservation. In the realm of real estate, this entails comprehensive property insurance, careful tenant selection, and proactive maintenance to safeguard against potential damage. In stocks and cryptocurrencies, understanding risk profiles, market trends, and having exit strategies in place are critical elements. The long-term perspective demands a disciplined approach to risk, acknowledging that temporary setbacks are part of the journey to enduring prosperity. The financial landscape is dynamic, and subject to shifts in market trends, economic climates, and regulatory frameworks. Regularly reviewing your investment portfolio is akin to recalibrating a compass on a journey – it ensures that your financial bearings align with your long-term goals. During these reviews, consider the performance of your real estate holdings, assess the health of your stock portfolio, and evaluate the resilience of your cryptocurrency investments. Adjustments made in response to changes in your financial situation or market conditions contribute to the sustained preservation of wealth. Preserving wealth over the long term demands more than static strategies; it requires an agile mindset informed by continuous financial education. Stay abreast of shifts in tax laws, emerging investment opportunities, and advancements in financial technology. In the realm of cryptocurrencies, where innovation is rapid, staying informed is particularly crucial. This commitment to ongoing learning equips you with the knowledge to adapt your wealth preservation strategy to the ever-evolving economic landscape. Life is marked by change, and your wealth preservation strategy must be adaptive to life's unfolding chapters. Marriage, the birth of children, career transitions — each life event necessitates a recalibration of your financial plan. Anticipate these changes and adjust your strategy accordingly. Estate planning becomes paramount during these life junctures, ensuring that your wishes for wealth distribution align with your evolving family dynamics. long-term wealth preservation transcends immediate gains; it's about safeguarding prosperity for the future. By embracing diversification, vigilant risk management, regular portfolio reviews, continuous financial education, and adaptability to life changes, you pave the way for a financial legacy that endures beyond your lifetime. As we progress, we will explore the path to realizing your financial goals, setting milestones, and maintaining the discipline needed to achieve real estate wealth through a well-rounded and sustainable approach to wealth management.

Chapter 9

THE PATH TO REAL ESTATE RICHES

Investing in real estate using stocks and crypto can be a rewarding and lucrative endeavor, but it also requires planning, strategy, and execution. Setting these goals not only provides a roadmap for your investment journey but also serves as the guiding star that aligns your aspirations with tangible, measurable outcomes. In this chapter, we will discuss some of the key steps and principles that can help you achieve your real estate investing goals and create lasting wealth. The foundation of setting financial goals lies in articulating clear and specific objectives. These objectives should be tailored to your unique financial situation, aspirations, and timelines. Whether it's acquiring investment properties, achieving a target portfolio value, or reaching a specific level of passive income, defining these objectives with precision is paramount. Setting measurable goals enables you to track progress and adjust strategies accordingly. For instance, instead of a vague goal like "owning real estate," a more specific goal could be "acquiring two rental properties within the next three years with a total annual rental income of $30,000." While financial goals are instrumental in wealth building, they should not exist in isolation. It's crucial to align these goals with your broader life aspirations. Consider how achieving these financial milestones contributes to your overall life plan. Whether it's providing for your family, funding educational pursuits, or ensuring a comfortable retirement, the synergy between financial goals and life aspirations creates a more meaningful and motivating framework. Not all financial goals hold the same level of urgency or significance. Prioritizing goals helps you allocate resources and effort effectively. Assess the short-term and long-term nature of your goals and determine which ones require immediate attention versus those that can be pursued over a more extended period. For example, if your primary goal is to accumulate a down payment for a real estate investment, prioritizing savings and exploring investment opportunities becomes paramount. On the other hand, a longer-term goal, such as achieving financial independence, might involve a more diversified investment strategy and a focus on long-term wealth preservation. The financial landscape is dynamic, and life circumstances evolve. Setting financial goals isn't a one-time task but an ongoing process that requires adaptability. Regularly reassess your goals considering changes in income, family situations, and market conditions. Flexibility in goal setting allows you to recalibrate your strategies, ensuring they remain relevant and achievable. As you set and pursue your financial goals, you lay the groundwork for a purposeful and successful journey toward leveraging stocks and crypto for real estate rich. It also includes Setting the Course: Defining Your Financial GPS. Before delving into the importance of tracking progress, it's crucial to recognize that setting clear financial goals acts as your financial GPS, guiding your every move. Establishing objectives that are specific, measurable, and time-bound provides a roadmap for your investments. Whether you aim to acquire real estate properties, build a diversified stock portfolio, or delve into the world of cryptocurrencies, defining these goals lays the foundation for your financial journey. Once your goals are established, the next step is to devise a set of Key Performance Indicators (KPIs) to measure your progress effectively. These KPIs serve as the metrics by which you gauge the health and growth of your investments. For stocks, this may include assessing portfolio growth, dividend yields, and stock performance. In real estate, you might track rental income, property appreciation, and overall real estate portfolio value. Cryptocurrency holdings could be measured by factors like portfolio value, returns on specific coins, and overall market performance. In the digital age, an array of financial tools and technology is at your disposal to streamline the tracking process. Online platforms, investment apps, and financial dashboards provide real-time insights into your portfolio's performance. Utilizing these tools not only simplifies the tracking process but also empowers you to make informed decisions based on accurate and up-to-date information. Tracking your progress is not a passive endeavor; it's an active and dynamic process that requires adaptability. Regularly reviewing your KPIs allows you to identify trends, anticipate challenges, and seize opportunities. If certain investments are consistently underperforming or if market conditions shift, you can adjust your strategies accordingly. Flexibility and adaptability are key elements in ensuring your financial journey remains aligned with your overarching goals. Beyond the tangible benefits of tracking progress, there is a profound psychological impact. Celebrating milestones along the way—whether it's reaching a certain portfolio value or acquiring a new property—provides a psychological boost. It fuels motivation, instills confidence, and acts as a reminder of the progress you've achieved. This psychological resilience becomes particularly crucial during challenging market conditions, as it reinforces your commitment to the long-term vision of real estate rich. Tracking your progress is not just a financial exercise; it's a strategic and psychological tool that propels you forward on the path to real estate riches. By setting clear goals, measuring your performance through KPIs, leveraging financial tools, adapting strategies based on insights, and celebrating milestones, you equip yourself with the tools needed to navigate the complexities of wealth building successfully.

The journey towards real estate rich is characterized by numerous achievements, both major and incremental. These milestones can take various forms, such as reaching a specific investment portfolio value, acquiring a new property, or achieving a targeted rate of return. Identifying these milestones requires a clear understanding of your financial goals and the steps necessary to attain them. Each milestone represents a significant step forward, propelling you closer to the realization of your real estate wealth objectives. Celebrating milestones offers more than just an opportunity to revel in success; it provides a moment for reflection. Taking time to acknowledge and appreciate the progress made reinforces the value of consistent effort and disciplined financial decision-making. Reflection is a powerful tool for learning, allowing investors to assess the strategies that led to success and apply those lessons to future endeavors. This introspection contributes to a more nuanced and informed approach to wealth building. Celebrating milestones serves as another powerful source of motivation in the challenging landscape of financial endeavors. As the path to real estate wealth is often characterized by peaks and valleys, maintaining motivation is essential for staying the course during inevitable market fluctuations and economic uncertainties. Milestone celebrations become a personal reward system, creating positive reinforcement for the discipline, effort, and strategic thinking invested in your financial journey. This motivation becomes a driving force, propelling you forward in the pursuit of even loftier goals. Celebrating milestones fosters a positive mindset, an invaluable asset in the world of wealth building. It transforms the narrative from a focus on challenges and obstacles to a recognition of accomplishments. A positive mindset is not just a product of success but a catalyst for future achievements. It instills confidence, resilience, and a belief in the ability to overcome hurdles. This mindset shift is instrumental in sustaining momentum and navigating the inevitable uncertainties that accompany financial endeavors. Beyond personal satisfaction, celebrating milestones contributes to the construction of a lasting legacy. Each milestone reached becomes a part of the narrative, a story of diligence, vision, and success. This legacy extends beyond the individual investor, influencing future generations and shaping a family's financial narrative. It establishes a tradition of wealth-building principles, demonstrating the rewards of strategic planning and disciplined execution.

Discipline and Patience are another context of financial success, which is the ability to endure without succumbing to the pressures of short-term market fluctuations. Markets, by their nature, are prone to volatility, with prices subject to the ebb and flow of economic cycles, geopolitical events, and investor sentiment. Patience involves maintaining a long-term perspective and understanding that the journey to real estate riches is a marathon rather than a sprint. In the world of real estate, the patience to wait for the right opportunities is paramount. Property markets may experience periods of rapid growth, followed by corrections. Patient investors understand that timing is crucial and resist the temptation to chase quick gains. They wait for favorable market conditions, conduct thorough due diligence, and make informed decisions aligned with their overall financial goals. Discipline complements patience by providing the structure and rigor necessary for effective wealth building. It involves adhering to a well-thought-out investment plan, even when faced with the allure of short-term gains or the fear induced by market downturns. Discipline requires staying true to your predetermined asset allocation, risk tolerance, and long-term objectives. In real estate, discipline manifests in various ways. It means resisting the urge to overextend financially, carefully evaluating potential investments, and not succumbing to market hype. Disciplined investors understand the importance of thorough research, robust risk management, and adherence to a set strategy. They recognize that successful real estate ventures are often the result of methodical planning and execution over time. Both patience and discipline become particularly crucial when navigating market volatility, a phenomenon inherent in both stocks and cryptocurrencies. Markets can experience rapid fluctuations, driven by a myriad of factors, from economic indicators to geopolitical events. During such times, patient and disciplined investors resist knee-jerk reactions. Instead, they view volatility as an inherent part of the investment journey, an opportunity to reassess and rebalance rather than a signal for panic. At the heart of both patience and discipline lies a long-term vision. Investors with real estate rich in their sights understand that wealth accumulation is not about making quick gains but about building a sustainable and resilient financial portfolio. This perspective allows them to weather short-term challenges, downturns, and market uncertainties with a calm demeanor, knowing that their strategy is grounded in a solid foundation. The role of patience and discipline in the path to real estate wealth cannot be overstated. These qualities empower investors to withstand the tests of time, market fluctuations, and unforeseen challenges. As you embark on your journey to leverage stocks and cryptocurrencies for real estate wealth, remember that it's not just about reaching the destination but also about the resilience and wisdom gained throughout the voyage. As we conclude this chapter, we will transition into the final section of the eBook, providing you with essential resources, tools, and actionable insights to empower you on your ongoing journey to leverage stocks and crypto for real estate rich.

Chapter 10

RESOURCES AND TOOLS FOR SUCCESS

In this final chapter, we'll provide you with a curated list of resources and tools to empower your journey to real estate rich. Whether you're seeking investment knowledge, mentorship, or tools for tracking your progress, these resources are invaluable for achieving success in your financial endeavors. In the interconnected world of finance and real estate, having access to reliable and up-to-date information is indispensable. Investment resources and websites act as your virtual mentors, offering a wealth of knowledge and analyses at your fingertips.

Bloomberg. A global leader in business and financial news, Bloomberg provides real-time market data, breaking news, and in-depth analyses of stocks, cryptocurrencies, and the broader financial landscape.

CNBC. Renowned for its comprehensive coverage of financial markets, CNBC delivers the latest news, interviews with industry experts, and insights into stock and crypto trends.

Reuters. A trusted source for unbiased news, Reuters covers financial markets, economic developments, and global events, helping you stay informed about factors influencing your investments.

Investment Platforms:

Investopedia. A comprehensive resource for investors of all levels, Investopedia offers articles, tutorials, and educational content covering a wide range of financial topics, including stocks, cryptocurrencies, and real estate.

Seeking Alpha. An excellent platform for stock market enthusiasts, Seeking Alpha provides stock analysis, market news, and a community of investors sharing their insights.

The Motley Fool. Known for its stock recommendations and investment advice, The Motley Fool offers a wealth of content to help you make informed investment decisions.

Real Estate Platforms

Zillow. A platform for real estate enthusiasts, Zillow provides property listings, market trends, and neighborhood information, allowing you to explore potential real estate investments.

Realtor. With a focus on property listings and market insights, Realtor.com is a valuable resource for real estate investors looking to stay updated on property values and trends. Redfin. Known for its user-friendly interface, Redfin offers a range of tools and information for homebuyers and real estate investors, including property research and market analyses.

Engaging with these resources enriches your understanding of market dynamics, investment strategies, and the latest developments in stocks, cryptocurrencies, and real estate. Regularly immersing yourself in financial news and analyses from these platforms ensures that you are well-equipped to make informed decisions. As you navigate the intricate world of real estate, these online resources become your constant companions, offering insights, research, and expert opinions. Consider them your virtual mentors, guiding you through market fluctuations, investment opportunities, and the nuances of financial decision-making. Remember, the journey to real estate rich is not only about the tangible assets you acquire but also about the knowledge and insights you accumulate along the way. Harness the power of these investment resources and websites to inform your decisions, refine your strategies, and ultimately achieve success in your financial endeavors. Embarking on a journey to real estate riches requires not only financial acumen but also a deep understanding of the principles that govern successful investing. Books serve as timeless companions, offering insights from seasoned investors and financial gurus. Here are a few must-reads that can significantly impact your investment journey: "The Millionaire Real Estate Investor" by Gary Keller: This classic offers a comprehensive guide to building wealth through real estate. Keller, co-founder of Keller Williams Realty, shares the strategies that successful investors employ to accumulate substantial real estate portfolios. "How the economics machine works in 30 minutes" by ray Dalio: A comprehensive guide on how the economics machine works in the act of finance and how money flows in and out as a transaction. "What I learned about losing a million dollars by Jim Paul and branded Moynihan: This compressive talk is about how an investor made millions of dollars and lost it in one day and how it worked on himself to make it back. "A Random Walk Down Wall Street" by Burton Malkiel: A comprehensive guide to various investment strategies, Malkiel's book explores the concept of efficient markets and emphasizes the merits of a diversified portfolio, providing readers with a holistic view of investment opportunities. While books offer valuable theoretical knowledge, courses provide a structured learning environment with practical applications. Here are some courses that can elevate your investment skills:

Real Estate Investment Courses on Udemy:

Udemy offers a plethora of real estate investment courses catering to all levels of expertise. From beginner guides to advanced strategies, these courses cover topics such as property analysis, financing, and risk management. "Financial Markets" on Coursera: Delivered by Yale University, this course provides an in-depth understanding of financial markets, including stocks and bonds. Professor Robert Shiller, a Nobel laureate in economics, shares insights into market dynamics and investment strategies. "Cryptocurrency Investment Course 2023: Fund Your Retirement!" on Udemy: As cryptocurrencies play an increasingly vital role in investment portfolios, this course provides practical guidance on investing in digital assets. It covers topics like blockchain technology, ICOs, and strategies for long-term growth. "Value Investing Bootcamp: How to Invest Wisely" on Udemy: Led by investment educator Nick Kraakman, this course delves into the principles of value investing. It covers essential concepts such as intrinsic value, margin of safety, and building a robust investment portfolio. Engaging with these recommended books and courses equips you with a diverse set of perspectives and practical skills. Remember that continuous learning is the cornerstone of successful investing, and these resources act as your mentors, guiding you toward the realization of your financial goals. As you absorb the wisdom contained within these pages and lectures, you'll find yourself better equipped to leverage stocks and crypto for the real estate rich you aspire to achieve.

CONCLUSION

As we have reached the final chapter of "how to leverage stocks and crypto for real estate rich," let's embark on a reflective journey, summarizing the pivotal lessons learned throughout this insightful exploration. The pages have been filled with strategies, principles, and wisdom aimed at empowering you in your pursuit of financial prosperity. Now, let's recap the key takeaways that will guide you as you navigate the exciting terrain of wealth-building through stocks, crypto, and real estate. A fundamental principle that echoes throughout the pages of this guide is the importance of diversification. Building a robust portfolio that spans stocks, cryptocurrencies, and real estate that acts as a shield against market volatility. Diversification is not merely a strategy; it's a philosophy that acknowledges the dynamism of financial markets and provides a guard against unforeseen challenges. In the ever-unpredictable world of finance, the pursuit of knowledge is a never-ending journey. The lessons from successful investors, the insights shared in recommended books, and the structured learning from courses are the building blocks of your financial education. Remember, every piece of information absorbed contributes to your ability to make informed decisions and navigate the complexities of your investment landscape. Discipline and emotional control emerge as committed companions in the realm of wealth building. Markets, whether real estate or crypto, are bound to experience fluctuations. The ability to maintain self-control, adhere to a well-thought-out strategy, and resist impulsive decisions is what separates successful investors from the crowd. Patience, discipline, and a long-term perspective are your allies on the path to wealth. Understanding the nuances of tax planning and wealth preservation is not just a safeguard—it's a strategy for generational success. The careful implementation of tax-efficient investment strategies and comprehensive estate planning ensures that the wealth you accumulate doesn't just grow but endures, leaving a legacy for your heirs. As you reflect on these key takeaways, envision your journey toward real estate riches as a dynamic, evolving process. Every decision you make, every piece of knowledge you acquire, and every experience you gain contributes to your financial growth. You are not merely an investor; you are the architect of your financial destiny. As you embark on a journey towards real estate, as a significant undertaking, and the decision to begin is a pivotal moment. Here's why you should take that first step with confidence: nothing happens without action. Your aspirations and dreams are powerful, but it is your actions that will translate them into tangible results. Getting started is the catalyst that propels you from compilation to execution. The most profound lessons are often learned through firsthand experience. By taking that initial step, you open the door to a world of practical knowledge. Each investment, success, or setback becomes a valuable lesson, contributing to your growth as an investor in confidence. Starting small allows you to build confidence gradually. As you witness your strategies yielding results, your confidence will grow. This newfound assurance will be your companion as you navigate the complexities of financial markets, real estate transactions, and cryptocurrency investments. Opportunities are abundant, but they favor those who are prepared to seize them. By getting started, you position yourself to recognize and capitalize on opportunities that align with your financial goals. Every successful investor starts with that first investment. Inactiveness, the resistance to change or motion, can be a powerful force. Taking that initial step breaks through inactivity, propelling you towards a future of financial independence and real estate richness. Momentum is a force that accelerates progress. The act of getting started generates momentum, creating a positive feedback loop that propels you forward. With each accomplishment, you build momentum, making subsequent steps easier and more rewarding. Picture your future yourself, reaping the rewards of the decisions you make today. The courage to start is a gift you give to your future self, providing the opportunity for financial security, freedom, and the realization of your dreams. Start by clarifying your financial goals, risk tolerance, and investment horizon. This will serve as your roadmap, guiding your decisions as you progress. Whether it's a modest investment in stocks, fractional ownership of real estate, or a small cryptocurrency purchase, take that first step. The size of the step is less important than the decision to move forward. The world of finance is dynamic, and continuous learning is the key to success. Stay curious, read, engage with communities, and evolve your strategies based on newfound knowledge. Do regularly monitor progress, adapt your strategies as needed, and celebrate milestones along the way. Recognize the significance of each step in your journey. Remember, the journey to real estate rich begins with a single step. Take that step with confidence, knowing that every action you take brings you closer to the financial future you aspire to achieve. Your journey awaits—seize it with passion and determination! At the core of realizing real estate wealth lies in the intersection between stocks, cryptocurrencies, and real estate. Each asset class brings its unique strengths to the table, and when strategically intertwined, they create a formidable wealth-building strategy. The compounding effect, an exponential growth fueled by reinvesting returns, is a force that comes alive when stocks, crypto, and real estate work in harmony. Stocks provide liquidity and growth potential, cryptocurrencies introduce the agility of digital assets, and real estate offers stability and tangible value that can be appreciated over time. Together, they form a dynamic triple capability of generating substantial wealth over the long term. Diversification is not merely a risk management strategy; it's a powerful tool for amplifying returns. Stocks, cryptocurrencies, and real estate often respond differently to market dynamics and economic conditions. By diversifying across these assets, you can mitigate risks associated with the volatility inherent in any one sector, creating a resilient portfolio that can weather various market conditions. The dynamic nature of the financial landscape presents a continuous flow of opportunities. Cryptocurrencies, with their transformative potential, bring a new dimension to wealth creation. Investing in real estate tokens, harnessing the benefits of blockchain technology in property transactions, and participating in the evolution of decentralized finance (defi) are just a few examples of the emerging opportunities that can propel your journey to real estate rich. Beyond the accumulation of wealth, the integration of stocks, crypto, and real estate facilitates effective wealth preservation and legacy building. Thoughtful tax strategies, estate planning, and a disciplined approach to long-term wealth management ensure that the wealth you accumulate endures across generations, creating a lasting legacy for your family. In the combination of stocks, crypto, and real estate, you hold the key to a wealth-building strategy that transcends the conventional. The potential for real estate rich isn't a distant dream; it's a tangible reality waiting to be unlocked by those who recognize the power of integration and strategic financial planning. As you embark on your journey to become real estate rich, remember that every step forward, no matter how small, is a step toward financial empowerment. Stay focused, stay informed, and stay committed. The potential for real estate riches with stocks and crypto is within your reach—seize it with confidence and determination. Best of luck on your path to financial success!

ABOUT THE AUTHOR

Tosin victor is a financial market analysis both investing and trader with a decade year of experience in technique analyst both stocks and crypto including new project investing, portfolio management, position trader, and Diversification. why create this book and what make it unique: because the dimension traditional path to financial freedom is no longer stand alone, it come with a compass of diversification, and find new opportunities at the right time, that is why have package full experience of how to build a diversify portfolio investment with stocks and crypto and used it for real estate wealth.